UNSEEN HANDS

&

UNKNOWN HEARTS

FOREWORD BY LILLIAN GONZALEZ-PARDO, M.D.

U N S E E N
H A N D S

&
U N K N O W N
H E A R T S

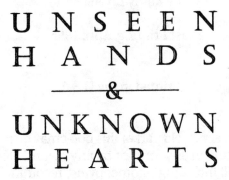

A MIRACLE OF HEALING
CREATED THROUGH PRAYER

KATHY L. CALLAHAN, PH.D.

A.R.E. Press • Virginia Beach • Virginia

A.R.E. Press
Sixty-Eighth & Atlantic Avenue
P.O. Box 656
Virginia Beach, VA 23451-0656

Library of Congress Cataloging-in-Publication Data
Callahan, Kathy L. (Kathy Lynn), 1953- .
    Unseen hands and unknown hearts : a miracle of healing cre-
ated through prayer / Kathy L. Callahan.
       p.   cm.
    ISBN 0-87604-330-9
    1. Aragon, Deirdre Lynette, 1980- . 2. Callahan, Kathy L. (Kathy
Lynn), 1953- . 3. Association for Research and Enlightenment—
Biography. 4. Reye's syndrome—Kansas—Patients—Biography.
5. Spiritual healing—Kansas—Case studies. 6. Prayer groups—
Kansas—Case studies. I. Title.
BP605.A77C35 1995
291.3—dc20   94-48787

Cover design by Richard Boyle

Dedication

This book is dedicated to my daughter, Deirdre Lynette Aragon, who made the selfless choice of beginning this journey so that others, by joining, might grow and learn; in loving memory of my father, Jerry Patrick Callahan, who met this life's journey with morale courage and fortitude, no matter the cost; and in loving memory of my aunt, Ida Vargo, whose entire life was a shining example of a journey well traveled.

TABLE OF CONTENTS

Acknowledgments

It is with deep gratitude that I wish to acknowledge the support and contributions of the following people:

To my husband, Tino, our daughter Deirdre, my sister Darcie Callahan, and Spirit Dog, thanks for your love and support. To my A.R.E. study group family: Brenda, Brad, and Sara Umholtz; Sharon Riley; Dot and Bill Kirklin; Jeanne, Rick, and Trish Aberill; and Joye McCallum and family; thanks for making this journey with me. To all of our relatives, especially Mary Louis and family; the Kie family; Ida Vargo; Cheryl, John, John, Jr., and Lisa Miller; John, Marylinn, Brett, Darren, and Lori Vargo; Rose Novak and family; Pat Davis and family; and Tom Yamayoshi; thanks for your love and prayers.

To the members of Unity Church of Overland Park, the A.R.E. Glad Helpers, Silent Unity, and the many healers who visited us at the hospital, thank you for your prayer power. You helped make a difference. To the Reverend Mary Omwake, thanks for being an angel of love. A special thank you to Tom Abate, whose unique gift of humor brought sunshine during our darkest hours.

To all those who visited at the hospital, please know that your daily support and words of encouragement helped see us through. Sincere thanks to my friends and co-workers—the staff and their families of Naval Reserve Readiness Command Region 18, and to Tino's friends and co-workers at Good Samaritan Nursing Home—Pat, Carol, Brian, Myrna, Dusty, and Diantha. We will never forget your many kindnesses.

To the many, many people across the country who in some way played a role in this journey, thank you for your prayers, meditations, rituals, and support. Know that it was *your* prayer that made this journey a miraculous one. Genuine thanks to the Knight family—Carolyn, Bob, Eric, Chris, and Beth—for your many cards and letters, to the office staff of Carolyn Greenes at Boston University, and to the staff and students at Rhein Benninghoven Elementary School.

A special thank you to the members of my new A.R.E. study group, Rita and John Baliunas; and Barbara and Jerry Lekstrom; for their support during the writing of this book and for their helpful insights in chapter 7. Thanks again to Brenda and Sharon for being a sounding-board for many of the ideas contained in these pages. Thank you to the members of my Stephen Ministry class, especially Elaine Rismiller, for their encouragement as I was writing, and to Lorita Armstrong ("Ta Ra") of Sedona, who helped me to see that "by not writing you are denying a part of yourself."

Thank you to my parents, Esther and Jerry. Thanks, Dad, for the example you set of burdens well carried. Thanks, Mom, for teaching me the reality of the unseen world.

A sincere thank you to my editor Jon Robertson and the staff of the A.R.E. Press for their guidance and for having the courage to take a chance on an unknown writer.

A most gracious and heartfelt thank you to the entire staff of the University of Kansas Medical Center (UKMC), to Dr. Enrique Chaves and Dr. Lillian Pardo, and particularly to the pediatric intensive care unit nurses, for their outstanding care, understanding, and support.

Finally, a humble thank you to the ever-abiding presence of Spirit, which guided me in the writing of this book.

Foreword

As science marched on to great discoveries and technologies, the art of medicine lagged behind. In the late 1970s the concept of mind/body medicine had its skeptics until Norman Cousins, through his writings and personal experience, gave new life to a principle that even Hippocrates and Galen recognized as important to health and healing. In 1993, Bill Moyers's *Healing and the Mind*[1] and its companion television series raised the consciousness of the world of medicine in those landmark works about the mind/body connection and how we think of sickness and health.

In the three decades that I have practiced medicine, I have learned that the higher the level of technology, the greater the need for the human touch. Science is about research and verifiable data, while the art of medicine is about caring, concern, and communication about what we know and what we don't know. And there is much more in medicine that we still do not know, even as new discoveries are made every day.

When patients and their families ask us about prognosis, such as what the future holds or what I refer to as "crystal ball" questions, physicians get very edgy, elusive, even evasive because of the inherent difficulties of the unknown. We become obligated to inform them of the spectrum of possibilities, from getting well to dying, but physicians who are trained to be healers and viewed as purveyors of hope can, nevertheless, be reluctant bearers of bad news, if indeed there are imminent signs of dying.

Cousins counseled physicians on the subject of prognosis: "The wise physician, when making a prognosis, does not confine himself or herself to the virulence of the particular microorganism involved or the nature of an abnormal growth; the wise physician makes a careful estimate of the patient's will to live and the ability to put to work all the resources of spirit that can be translated into beneficial biochemical changes." He further said, "Among recent discoveries in the practice of medicine is the fact that human beings come equipped with resources for healing that are best mobilized not by detached scientific efficiency, but by communication and supportive human outreach."[2]

It has often been said that while there is life there is hope, but hope springs eternal only in the hearts of those who believe. This book is the story of Deirdre and her family who fervently hoped, prayed, and believed in the return of

Deirdre to health and happiness. As the other person on the other side of this "miracle," I understood that science did only what it could do, then art took over, as reflected in the cultural values and beliefs of her family and their community of friends. They never gave up and encouraged others in similar predicaments not to give up, they uplifted spirits and willed for recovery and life.

Every episode, experience, or endeavor carries a message, a moral lesson, or a learning opportunity. In my academic life as a student, a teacher, and as an example for others, there is a rule I have followed—learn one new thing each day, the "pearl-a-day" philosophy. If we follow this precept, we would have several strings of pearls as we go through our life on earth. And so what is the message of this book? There are lessons to be learned for everyone. Let me count the ways!

For Deirdre, she knows she is a very special person, she was "chosen" to carry forth the reasons for her being in this world. She also considers herself very lucky, a precious jewel to her family and friends. She was given a second chance and will continue her academic interest that was interrupted by her illness, and she will gather her own pearls along the way.

For Deirdre's parents, Kathy and Tino, their spiritual work will continue and will benefit others as we begin to understand the processes of healing that go beyond science; their gratitude for bringing their precious daughter to health and well-being, and for Kathy the determination to share with others through her journalistic talents the spiritual and cultural values that are essential but often overlooked in our lives.

For physicians at all levels of their professional development—students, residents, and practitioners, both generalists and specialists—this book reminds us to be faithful to the science, but not to forget the art of medicine. Learn from the rich experiences of life as you practice your profession.

It is still a very noble one, despite politics, economics, and reform.

For the public, consumers and patients, whose desires and demands for technologies as part of their health care seem uncontrolled and unabated—the search for diagnosis and a cure exists not in those high technological systems alone, but you must help yourself by allowing health promotion and disease prevention programs; and no matter what your creed, color, or ethnicity, believe in the human spirit and its power.

The West has met with the East; some consensus and collaboration of their philosophies have evolved from the meeting of their minds. Hope springs eternal, as art and science together march onward.

Lillian Gonzalez-Pardo, M.D.
Clinical Professor in Pediatrics and Neurology
University of Kansas Medical Center

Prologue

Spirit in Action

*The Journey itself creates the warrior; daily life is your
journey and is the means of your training.*
                    —Dan Millman, *No Ordinary Moments*

THIS is the story of a spiritual journey that began in pain
and sorrow, and that many thought would end in death. Our
journey was neither expected nor welcomed. It was perhaps
the most difficult trial we have ever been asked to endure.
Those of us who walked this path believe that we have an obli-
gation to share it with others. It is, however, but one of many
roads. As you join in our journey, it is my hope that you will
take with you what you find valuable and useful in your life.

The Crossroads of Crisis

The most harrowing fear that any one can imagine is a crisis that affects the welfare of a loved one. A missing teen, a parent suffering from a chronic disease, a spouse suddenly injured, or a child stricken with an acute illness are nightmare-like ordeals that no one wants to believe can happen to him or her. The helplessness and desolation that you feel can be fully understood only by those who have experienced a similar misfortune. You stand by, helpless, and watch as your loved one fights for life, knowing there is nothing you can do to help, feeling despair to a depth you had never thought possible.

Definitions of the word "crisis" underscore the idea that a crisis is a "turning point,"[1] a decisive state of things, precipitated by unanticipated circumstances, which can have either positive or negative consequences. In medicine, a crisis is defined as the turning point in the course of a disease, which indicates recovery or death. The Chinese language offers an excellent example also of the idea of crisis as a turning point or crossroads. Its pictograph for "crisis" is made from a combination of two written characters: The first character means "danger" and the second means "opportunity." In this sense, a crisis presents either an opportunity to grow or the danger of decline.

As parents, my husband, Tino, and I found ourselves in the middle of such a crisis when our daughter, Deirdre, at the age of ten, was suddenly stricken with a life-threatening disease. The terror we felt when we heard the diagnosis and the panic that followed are something we will never forget. They are ingrained into our very being. Our immediate reaction was one of shock and disbelief, which left us immobilized, unable to think clearly or comprehend the meaning of what was happening. As the reality of the situation slowly sank in, feelings of fear and helplessness grew. It was as if the very fabric which held our lives together had been suddenly rent at the seams, destroyed to such an extent that it might never be whole again.

AT THE CROSSROADS

When standing at such a crossroads, you rarely think to logically consider the options before you. More often, emotions dominate your thoughts and you think with your heart. We knew that stories of miraculous happenings are by no means unusual. In fact, both inspirational literature and medical case histories cite many examples of people who, despite severe physical and mental handicaps, overcome great obstacles and beat the odds. Health crises or natural disasters often serve as the setting for miracles, because in these situations people are forced to join together to overcome harrowing circumstances. The ability of the human spirit to triumph over seemingly impossible physical conditions cannot be denied.

We also knew that in such so-called "miracles" two themes are apparent. The first is the ability, on the part of those who experience them, to view any circumstance as an opportunity for growth or the ability to turn "obstacles" into "stepping-stones." The second is a belief in the existence of a Higher Power or spiritual force greater than oneself, along with the belief that the creative energy of this Higher Power can be made manifest on earth. The name for this Higher Power may be Father-God, Mother-God, Jehovah, Christ, Allah, Buddha, Krishna, or any other of the myriad names humans have given to this universal power. For purposes of this book, all of these will be considered manifestations of the one Creative Force or Spirit.[2]

A miracle can be said to occur when the creative energy of Spirit is consciously applied for the purpose of creating a positive change on the physical plane. An event is considered to be a miracle because the final outcome defies physical laws and expectations.

When Deirdre first became ill, however, our only thought was of the immediate situation and finding a way to save her life. Our daughter was dying, and we were willing to try anything to prevent her death. We had no great plan or purpose other than to help her get well. Initially, we did what most people do when their child falls desperately ill—pray, rely upon spiritual beliefs, and call upon family and friends for support.

A FAITH IN GOD, A BELIEF IN SPIRIT

For many years, Tino and I sought to understand spiritual principles through the study of metaphysics.[3] The main premise of metaphysics is that all physical or material conditions are manifestations of spirit or energy. Spirit (thought or idea) is the cause; the physical (material condition) is the effect. I believe that although people do not always think of ideas as being "metaphysical," many individuals are actually familiar with these concepts. For example, well-known proverbs such as "What goes around comes around" and "It's just a case of mind over matter" have their root meanings firmly grounded in metaphysical thought. Simply put, they each say that everything we see in the physical world first begins with an idea. Whatever enters into our lives is the "material expression" of a mental equivalent we hold.[4]

The recent phenomenon of the "new age" movement has resulted in a resurgence of metaphysical ideas in America. This term is misleading, however, for few of these ideas are new. In fact, most of these ideas are very ancient concepts. The philosophy of metaphysics has existed for thousands of years and transcends time, religion, and culture. Metaphysical thought can be found in many Eastern religious texts, including works on the Tao, Buddhism, and Hinduism; in writings of Western philosophers such as Plato, Socrates, and Aristotle; and even within the Judeo-Christian tradition.[5]

Interestingly, the current heightened interest in metaphysics has been bolstered by recent scientific discoveries. The medical profession, for example, is giving increased credence to the idea that there is a definite link between mind and body. It is now accepted that a person's mental and emotional status (thought or idea) has a definite effect upon the individual's recovery from disease or injury (physical condition). Holistic health practices, which have only played a minimal role in traditional medical care, are gaining acceptance as viable alternative treatments.

As a teen, I had started studying the metaphysical concepts found in the Edgar Cayce psychic readings. Edgar Cayce[6] is perhaps America's best-known psychic. Born in Kentucky in 1877, he had the ability to enter a trance state and access information not available through the five senses. This gift came to light in 1898, when during hypnosis, he described the cause of and cure for his chronic laryngitis. From that time on, until his death in 1945, Cayce gave over 14,000 psychic "readings." More than 9,000 deal with the physical ailments of people who wrote or came to him for help; they include causes of and suggested treatments for these problems. Their accuracy continues to amaze those who study them. The remaining readings were given in response to questions on religious and spiritual issues, metaphysics, history, and future events.

The readings constitute one of the largest documented records of psychic perception and have been cross-indexed under thousands of subject headings, computerized, and made available for study through the efforts of the Association for Research and Enlightenment, Inc. (A.R.E.). Founded in 1931, the A.R.E. is a nonprofit, open membership organization committed to spiritual growth, holistic healing, psychical research, parapsychology, and metaphysical studies.

In recent years, I had expanded my interests to include other metaphysical writings in addition to the Cayce readings. A lifelong member of the Lutheran church (Evangelical Lutheran Church in America), I had little trouble integrating these beliefs with a traditional Christian upbringing. I saw them as a complement to, rather than a contradiction of, mainstream Christianity.

Tino is of Native American heritage, a full-blooded Laguna Pueblo, who was reared on the Laguna Pueblo reservation in New Mexico. Over the years, he combined his traditional spiritual beliefs with other metaphysical teachings. In the two years preceding Deirdre's illness, he had become increasingly interested in the teachings of the Unity School of Christianity, which was founded in 1889 by Charles and Myrtle Fillmore. It began as a spiritual movement to help people in the practical application of the eternal Truths as taught by Jesus Christ. It professes no strict creed or dogma, but presents a practical philosophy for living life in alignment with universal laws. Today, Unity congregations are found throughout the world and carry on an active prayer ministry.

As a married couple, Tino and I have often shared our thoughts, opinions, and questions on spiritual matters and felt that we were trying to apply spiritual principles in our everyday lives.

There was nothing unusual about our lives. We were facing the same highs and lows, joys and sorrows as anyone else as we dealt with the experiences of everyday life. There were birthdays to celebrate, joy at Christmas as family was reunited, and milestones to mark in our daughter's life. There were unexpected career changes, financial difficulties, and problems on the job. Some plans we had made came to fruition; others did not.

Throughout all the ups and downs that life brings, we tried to hold fast to the belief, expressed so well by Gary Zukav in his book *Seat of the Soul*, that everything that happens in our lives occurs for a reason and provides us with a learning opportunity. Zukav refers to living on earth as being in "earth school."[7] Each experience is an opportunity to learn a lesson that will enhance spiritual growth. If the lesson is handled correctly, it results in a closer union with God. If it's handled incorrectly, class remains in session and the lesson is repeated until it is learned. An underlying belief to this concept is that God, as our Father and Creator, wants only the best for us. " . . . for it is your Father's good pleasure to give you the kingdom" (Luke 12:32 RSV), and the experiences we encounter are always in the interest of our highest good.

Having already accepted these principles as true, the challenge for us, even before Deirdre became ill, was to apply them in daily life. At times it was easy, at other times hard, and in a few instances it was nearly impossible. Hindsight, as they say, is a wonderful teacher, and upon reflection it always did appear that no matter how awful the situation seemed to be at the time, the end result *was* in our best interest.

Our beliefs, however, were to face their severest test as our daughter was diagnosed with Reye's syndrome, a life-threatening disease. How could this situation be in our best interest? What lesson could possibly be learned from this? How could a loving God subject us to such pain? These were only some of the questions that haunted us as we tried to make sense of our situation. Did God really expect us to believe, even now?

ON THE ARM OF ANOTHER

Maintaining one's faith in the midst of such a crisis is not an easy matter. No matter how deep your faith may be, questions of doubt continue to plague you, and you quickly realize that this is something you cannot do alone. Making it through a crisis requires a cooperative effort that only a support system can provide. The necessity of relying on a support system cannot be overemphasized.

Fortunately, Tino and I were not alone. We were supported not only by family and friends, but by hundreds of people who joined in a spontaneous, interdenominational prayer network that involved dozens of religious groups and stretched from coast to coast, and even to Hawaii.

A Search for God Study Group

As a longtime member of the Association for Research and Enlightenment, Inc. (A.R.E.), I was well aware of the existence of Search for God study groups. These study groups, which exist throughout the world, are composed of individuals who have an interest in discussing the spiritual principles found in the Edgar Cayce readings. The group meets weekly at a member's home and provides both a nonjudgmental atmosphere and a framework of support as participants try to *live* according to the universal laws and apply them in daily life. Yet despite the many positive comments I had heard about study group membership, I was an A.R.E. member for more than twenty years before I took action and joined my first group in 1989.

At the time I joined, my initial reason was the severe obstacle I was experiencing in what I considered an intolerable situation in my career. It was getting more and more difficult for me to apply spiritual principles as I knew I should, and I felt I needed the advice and encouragement a study group might provide. Looking back on it, I realize that I had actually been led to this group for more far-reaching reasons as well, for I realize now that it was necessary that our group be together as a unit prior to Deirdre's illness because of the learning opportunity we would have to experience *together*. It was as if we had come together, at the appointed place and time, to join in a spiritual journey as perhaps we had done in the distant past.

The study group I was drawn to had been in existence for over twenty years and had seen changes in membership as well as in location. During the two years of my association with it, we had all become close friends. Indeed, as with many study groups, we were more like family in many ways. Active group members at that time included: Dot and Bill Kirklin (who were the original founders), Brenda Umholtz, Sharon Riley, Jeanne Aberill, and Joye McCallum. Several of our children often accompanied us to meetings, including Brenda's daughter Sara, Jeanne's daughter Trish, and, of course, Deirdre. Brenda's husband, Bradley (Brad), and Tino also attended meetings from time to time, so we were well acquainted with one another's families. When Deirdre became ill, these people became our support system.

Angel of Love

During the autumn preceding Deirdre's illness, I had been seeking to join a new church. The church we had been attending was experiencing some difficulties, and the Sunday school was folding. I had decided that I must look for a new church "for Deirdre," a church which I hoped would provide her with a firm spiritual foundation. It was not until much later that I would come to realize the true prophetic meaning of those words.

Following a suggestion from Tino, I paid a visit to the Unity Church of Overland Park, Kansas, near our home in Shawnee, Kansas, where we were living at the time. It was the first time I had ever considered joining other than a Lutheran church, and I was not sure what to expect. After my first visit, however, I knew I had "come home." My reaction was similar to the feeling frequently described by others. The sense of peace, harmony, and love this church engenders is difficult to put into words. Although God is everywhere present, many people experience an extremely strong sense of the Lord's presence upon entering that sanctuary. As with many others before me, this feeling of oneness, serenity, and love stayed with me and helped to sustain me as I went about my business throughout the week.

It was an easy decision to begin attending this church on a regular basis. Deirdre participated in the Sunday school classes, and within two months she was an assistant in the nursery during church services. The joy and fulfillment she received as she cared for the little ones was readily apparent. We were happy to become members of the Unity family.

The strong sense of God this church radiates was due in large part to the presence of the senior minister, Reverend Mary Omwake. Mary is a person who is totally centered in love, the *agape* sense of universal love as taught by the Christ. This sense of love and this unity of spirit permeate all that she undertakes. I think of her as an angel of love, living the true meaning of the Christ Spirit which seems to radiate in and through her. Her presence later at the hospital during Deirdre's illness would prove to be invaluable.

Spiritual Tools

We believe that Spirit is aware of our path even before we embark upon it and works to ensure that we learn all we may one day need to know. God knows our self-imposed limits and our true potential far better than we ourselves. And though God may stretch us beyond our own self-limiting expectations, we will never be asked to enter a situation unprepared or accept a greater burden than we can bear.

Knowledge of many of the tools my family and friends would use on our journey came from many years of studying the metaphysical concepts presented in the Edgar Cayce readings, particularly the universal or spiritual laws of prayer, faith, and love. Spiritual laws[8] are divine laws that were put into motion by God for the purpose of guiding us on our individual journey back to oneness with Him. They are immutable, in continuous operation, and affect us whether or not we are aware of their existence. Awareness of these laws and their meaning, however, can help us to discover our purpose in life and find the way back to our spiritual source.

Awareness of additional tools we would use came through my enrollment in "Unity Basics" just six weeks prior to my daughter's illness. This course was a first-time offering, and its purpose was to teach spiritual principles and demonstrate practical ways to apply those principles in daily life. The lessons focused on the power of thought (spiritual energy) and its ability to affect the physical world. It included the use of denials and affirmations, the application of positive scientific prayer, and exercising the power of the spoken word.

I soon realized that the concepts I was learning in class were closely related to many ideas advocated in the Edgar Cayce readings, and I eagerly shared this information with the study group. Although the Unity class had already commenced, Brenda and Sharon both felt compelled to join. Informed that the class had already exceeded maximum enrollment, Brenda did something totally out of character and rather aggressively pushed the issue. Her persistence paid off, however, for she and Sharon received special permission to enroll in the course.

An interesting aspect of this class was the warning or admonition—that the students received—to be cautious. We were informed that the material being presented had great potential to create change if correctly applied. The warning, however, was to beware of what you ask for. If you ask for transformation in your life, it will come, *because Truth does work!* Opportunities for transformation, however, will occur in accordance with our highest good and not necessarily with our wishes. "Hang on to your hats," we were cautioned, "and prepare for a roller coaster ride that will change your life."

Undaunted, we were asking for transformation in our

lives and were eagerly anticipating opportunities for change in such areas as health, work environment, personal relationships, and financial prosperity. Despite the warning that opportunity often knocks in unexpected ways, neither I nor Sharon nor Brenda could have possibly imagined the way in which it would manifest.

PROMISES AND MIRACLES

In addition to the support we received in our families and friends, many of us found hope and encouragement in the words and promises of Jesus the Christ.[9] The Gospel lessons and Sunday school stories I had learned as a child quickly came to mind and helped sustain me. The legacy He left us in parables and promises is not only rhetoric, but provides a blueprint for action if we but *apply* these teachings.

The comfort many of us took in Christ's words found a complementary counterpart in the writings of *A Course in Miracles*.[10] In the year preceding Deirdre's illness, four study group members had, within a short time, independently discovered the *Course*. Despite our sometimes mixed emotions, the consensus was that overall its material complemented many of the ideas set forth in the Cayce readings.

The information in the *Course* is inspired writing received by Helen Schucman, then a professor of medical psychology at Columbia University's College of Physicians and Surgeons in New York City. In 1965, Helen and a colleague, William "Bill" Thetford, decided to find a more loving and accepting way of dealing with the problems plaguing their medical department. As if in response, Helen began to receive information in the form of a voice identifying itself as the Christ. "This is a course in miracles," the voice said. "Please take notes."

Helen's initial reaction was one of dismay and disbelief. Of Jewish heritage, she described herself as a "psychologist, educator, conservative in theory, and atheistic in belief." Yet with Bill's help and encouragement they began to write down the information she was given. This continued for seven years and resulted in a set of three books which comprise the *Course*. It has been a source of controversy in some corners and its merits will most likely be debated for years. I must admit that I can understand the ambivalence the *Course* engenders, for there were times when I wanted to take the book and throw it at the wall, never to look at it again. Yet, there were other times when I felt that the Christ Presence itself was speaking to me through the words written on its pages.

Its main teaching is that the way to remember God is by undoing guilt through forgiveness of others. Of the multitude of lessons it presents, however, five concepts would prove to have been the useful tools we needed on our journey: (1) miracles are the natural order of things, (2) creation is an extension of God, an extension of love, (3) only that created by God (the spiritual) is real, (4) the physical world and its conditions are but projections of what we think we see; the physical is an illusion which can be changed when we change our perception, and (5) change at the physical level can be instantaneous.

A Step of Choice

And so began our journey. A life-threatening illness would force us to the crossroads of crisis. During the first hours of Deirdre's illness, Tino and I discussed our situation with the other members of our study group. Dark clouds of doubt seemed to hang over us and we were confused. We wanted to believe that a miracle would save her, but did we dare to hope for such a thing? Or should we come to terms with the situation and accept the idea that Deirdre might die? Was the lesson to be learned, perhaps, in our acceptance of her death? Or would acceptance of the situation mean that we were giving up and not having faith in the power of Spirit? Would this choice mean that we were accepting the illness as a stumbling block rather than trying to transform it into a stepping-stone? Should we try to look beyond the physical illusion of Deirdre's illness and acknowledge the reality of Spirit to change it? Did we dare believe that we could help bring about a miracle? What if we tried to do this and failed? What if we applied everything we thought to be true and Deirdre died anyway? Finally, we faced questions, such as what would happen to our faith and beliefs if that occurred? When should we hold on to hope and when should we let go and let God?

These were but a few of the many questions we faced as Deirdre's story unfolded. Day by day, hour by hour, we struggled to solve the complexities of the issues which confronted us. Although we did make a step of choice, we had no way of knowing what the final outcome would be until we lived through each and every agonizing minute of our journey.

● ● ●

I have been driven many times to my knees by the overwhelming conviction that I had nowhere else to go.
—Abraham Lincoln

In February of 1991, we rushed our ten-year-old daughter, Deirdre, to a hospital emergency room after she became disoriented and incoherent during what had appeared to be a routine bout of flu. Within two hours, she was diagnosed with Reye's syndrome, a life-threatening disease with a high mortality rate. There is no cure, only a course of treatment that has proved successful in some cases. As she became comatose, we knew we were facing the worst crisis of our lives. The days passed with no improvement; her brain activity lessened. The medical prognosis went from "little hope" to "hopeless." Many times we had said the words, "I believe." But now, as our daughter's life hung in the balance, would we be able to put that belief into action? God was asking us to grow beyond acceptance on an intellectual level, put faith and knowledge into action, and believe from the heart.

PART I:

MIRACLE IN
THE MAKING

1

The Journey Begins

... the thing which I greatly feared is come upon me, and
that which I was afraid of is come unto me.   —Job 3:25

Beginnings

FEBRUARY 1991 was a very busy month in our household. My daughter, Deirdre, was hard at work on a science project for her school's annual science fair. It was the first year that she, as a fifth grader, could enter a project. She was determined to not only win a first-place blue ribbon, but she had decided that her project was going to be one of ten projects selected for entry in the regional Research & Development (R&D) Forum. All fifth-grade students were required to submit projects, and she would be competing with approximately ninety students.

All of the experimental work had to be conducted in the classroom during school hours. There were many long nights of work at home, too, as she analyzed the results of the experiment, wrote a research paper, and prepared an elaborate presentation board for display. Having no computer, she had to do the work on a typewriter and use stencils, construction paper, and the old cut-and-paste method to prepare the display board. She was very excited about her project and was eagerly awaiting the day of the science fair.

February was also a busy month for me as Desert Shield became Desert Storm, and the entire country turned its attention to the conflict in the Middle East. The focus at our house was intensified by the fact that I was an officer in the U.S. Navy. I had spent the previous six months actively involved in the recall and mobilization of reservists. The command's normal working hours had expanded into long nights and twenty-four-hour watches. With the majority of reservists having been recalled the month prior, our task was winding down. I still had a keen interest in the conflict, however, for I was acquainted with both naval reservists and active duty sailors assigned to the area. As the offensive was launched, our television became the focal point of many an evening, as we anxiously followed events. Little did we know that in a few days we would be fighting a war of our own in a hospital waiting room.

Complicating the hectic activity of February was a regional outbreak of a severe influenza virus. During the week of the science fair, one-third of the students were absent due to the flu, another third was recovering, and the remaining students were beginning to show symptoms. My daughter fell into this latter group. Five days prior to the science fair, Deirdre began to complain of a sore throat and to run a slight fever. She had always been a healthy child, having the flu only once before in all her ten years. Even when she had the chicken pox she was not overly ill; in fact, she viewed that week as a vacation from school and showed little of the usual malaise associated with the disease. She had the normal colds and sore throats from time to time, but I considered myself fortunate that God had blessed me with such a healthy child.

Despite a low-grade fever and sore throat, Deirdre insisted on putting the finishing touches on her science project. She worked many hours each day after school to ensure that everything was perfect. After all, she reminded me, her project was going to be selected for the R&D Forum. I told her I was very proud of her for continuing to work despite the fact that she wasn't feeling well.

The day of the science fair finally arrived, but the anticipated excitement was dampened by the fact that Deirdre's symptoms had worsened. I wanted to keep her home and told her that I would take her project to school. She insisted on going herself so that she could set it up, and there was no talking her out of this. I agreed to let her go, but told her to see the school nurse, if necessary. She did see the nurse later that morning, and when her father picked her up at school, she was one of some twenty students who were being sent home and were waiting for their parents. Like Deirdre, others had insisted on going to school that day so that they could set up their projects.

By evening, she was too ill to even think about attending the evening session of the science fair that was open to the public. I went to view the projects and to find out the results of the closed judging that had taken place that afternoon. Much to my delight, her project had received a first-place blue ribbon. As I talked with her teacher, I informed her that Deirdre would not be back to school that week. Her teacher told me that selections for the R&D Forum were being kept confidential and wouldn't be publicly announced until the next day. Then she took me aside and whispered that since

Deirdre wouldn't be in school to hear the announcement, she could tell me that her project had indeed been selected. She said she knew just how hard Deirdre had worked on the project and felt that she should know because it might help her get well more quickly. Arriving home, I awoke Deirdre and told her the news. She was happy, but was too sick to enjoy the moment and could barely stay awake to hear what I had to say. Telling her that sleep was the best medicine, I tucked her in, knowing that tomorrow we had an appointment with our family doctor, Dr. Joel Feder.

Throughout the night, Deirdre would occasionally cry out that her stomach was hurting her.

"Mommy, make the hurt go away," she repeated. "Why does it have to hurt so much?"

As any parent would, I asked the usual questions about where the pain was and what it felt like, but there was nothing to indicate that she was suffering from anything other than a routine bout of the flu. She didn't want to be left alone, so I lay down beside her. I felt badly that I couldn't do anything to lessen her pain, and I tried to comfort her by telling her that we would see our doctor tomorrow and reassure her that he would be able to help her get well. It was a long night.

While at his office the next day, Dr. Feder conducted the standard tests. As always, he made a thorough physical examination and wanted to test both urine and blood. When the nurse tried to draw a blood sample, however, Deirdre became hysterical. She screamed, fought, and jumped whenever the needle entered her arm. The doctor and I both tried to hold her down, but after three attempts the two nurses were unsuccessful. This behavior was unusual for Deirdre, but the doctor attributed it to her illness. Rather than cause her any more stress, he decided to forgo the blood test. The results of the other tests were all within normal limits for a child suffering from the flu, and he had seen dozens of similar cases in the last few weeks. He prescribed an anti-emetic in suppository form to reduce the vomiting, told us to make sure she got plenty of rest and fluids, and to call him if there were any changes.

I left for home thinking that my daughter, like hundreds of other children, was suffering from the effects of a "normal" flu virus. There was nothing to indicate that this was anything more than a routine bout of flu, and there was no reason to suspect that within hours her illness would take a drastic turn for the worse.

Once home, Tino and I gave Deirdre a dose of the medication. Following our doctor's suggestion, we gave her an initial double dose. Then we put her to bed, telling her that rest would help the medicine work better. The vomiting did seem to decrease during the next several hours, although she continued to complain of stomach pain.

By early evening, Deirdre had awakened and joined us as we were watching television. Her complaints about the stomach pain continued.

"Mommy, it hurts. Make it go away," she repeated over and over again.

There was nothing I could do to comfort her. After holding her for about an hour, I helped her back to bed. Walking upstairs with her, I realized she seemed a little disoriented. She had walked right over some plants we kept on the staircase. Tucking her into bed, I again told her that sleep was the best medicine and that she needed to try to rest. Her father came to sit with her while I went to sleep on the living room sofa. Although it was a Friday night, I had to be at work early the next morning for a duty weekend.

A short time later, I was awakened by her cries. Tino told me that she had become increasingly restless and was tossing about in bed. Her fever was elevated, so we gave her a cool sponge bath. This seemed to help, for she quieted down and asked to go back to bed. Tino continued his vigil and I went back to sleep. It wasn't very long before her cries began again.

Suddenly, through my half-awake state, I heard Tino calling me.

Struggling to wake up completely, I felt a strange feeling sweep over me. With a jolt I sat upright, experiencing a flash of insight. Fear welled up in my throat, for I suddenly knew what had happened.

"Tino," I shouted. "Ask her where she is! Ask her where she is," I called, for the terrible feeling was telling me that my daughter was no longer in her body. Somehow I knew she had gone.

Running up the stairs, I found Tino holding Deirdre in a sitting position. Her head rolled from side to side. Shouting her name and tapping her cheek, I got no response. Her eyes appeared glazed and unfocused. Without hesitation, we hastily prepared to rush Deirdre to the hospital. I got the car ready, while Tino carried Deirdre down two flights of stairs to the garage. He had difficulty navigating the narrow stairwell, her body feeling like "dead weight." Laying her in the back seat, we headed for the nearest hospital, only five minutes away.

By now, Tino and I were beginning to think that she might be having a reaction to the medication. We had both worked in medical settings and were somewhat familiar with drug reactions. We discussed the possibility that perhaps the initial double dose had been too much. If that was the problem, it was something that could be quickly dealt with and, although serious, Deirdre would soon be well. We were sure that it couldn't be anything more threatening than that.

EMERGENT CRISIS

We arrived at the emergency room of Shawnee Mission Medical Center around 1:00 a.m. Saturday morning. Rushing inside, I told the duty nurse that my daughter was in the car, semiconscious, and that we needed help to bring her inside. Immediately, attendants appeared with a gurney, lifted her out of the car, and wheeled her into an examination room. Tino stayed with Deirdre, while I gave the required admission information to the receptionist.

Deirdre quickly became the focus of a flurry of activity. Initial vital signs were taken and a thorough examination begun. She appeared to be "semiconscious," meaning that although she did not respond to verbal or visual stimuli, she was responding to touch and pain. As the examination continued, her restlessness increased and she appeared to make involuntary, erratic movements. She fought attempts by a nurse to insert an i.v., and Tino and I had to help hold her down while it was inserted. Within minutes, Deirdre reached over with her free hand and tore the i.v. from her arm. I watched as blood squirted in all directions, the needle ripping her skin. More nurses appeared, attending the wound and trying to help restrain her. Tino and I again struggled to hold her down as the nurses inserted yet another i.v., this time securing it to her arm with a board and putting light restraints on her arms.

By now, Deirdre had begun to bite, rotating her head in all directions, attempting to catch anything in her teeth. As Tino leaned over her chest while the second i.v. was inserted, she swung her head around and sunk her teeth into his arm. The teeth marks went through his heavy leather jacket and caused an ugly bruise that would take weeks to heal. If it hadn't been for the thickness of the jacket, her teeth would have pierced his skin.

Even though Deirdre was tied down with light restraints, her combative behavior continued. A nurse tried repeatedly to insert a catheter to obtain a urine sample, but each attempt brought more resistance. Unable to proceed any further, the nurse called for a security guard. Between the three of us, we barely managed to hold her still enough for the catheter to be inserted. The security guard commented that he couldn't believe a little girl could be so strong.

It was around this time that the screaming began. Without warning, Deirdre began to emit a shrill, high-pitched cry or shriek. She would scream when someone touched her and at other times she would cry out without provocation. As her screams escalated, the fear I was feeling escalated as well, and I watched her erratic behavior with growing anxiety.

As the medical team continued to work on Deirdre, Tino and I answered many questions regarding her condition and the events leading up to this point. As if the strain of the last few hours wasn't enough, we had to repeat the same information every time a new doctor or nurse appeared. Upon hearing that Deirdre had been examined by our family doctor only hours earlier, they immediately called him to discuss his findings. The medical team seemed to be having a hard time believing that her condition could have changed so rapidly. They were also concerned about illicit drug use, although I assured them that that was not possible. The only drug she had taken was the Compazine® prescribed by our doctor. That had to be the reason for this reaction.

Not much more than an hour after admittance, a doctor called me out of the room and over to the nurses' station. Based upon the results of the tests, he had a preliminary diagnosis.

"I don't want to alarm you," he began, "but we could be facing a very serious situation. We believe there is a good possibility your daughter has Reye's syndrome."

Reye's syndrome! The words continued to echo in my mind. I didn't hear much of what he said after that. I had read about Reye's syndrome in a *Reader's Digest* article some years before. Memory told me that it was a killer disease, a leading cause of death in young children. Those who did survive often suffered severe brain damage or paralysis.

Reye's syndrome! I was totally unprepared for anything of this magnitude. A bad case of the flu, a drug reaction, yes. But not this. This doctor was telling me that my daughter might die! I could not and did not want to comprehend the meaning of what he was saying. His words echoed in my head, but I did not hear them. I lost all sense of time and thought.

I vaguely recall the doctor talking about elevated levels of something in her urine, which was characteristic of the disease and had led to the diagnosis. He told me she would have to be transferred to another hospital, a hospital equipped with a special pediatric unit capable of dealing with these cases. He mentioned several possibilities, but I couldn't think clearly to choose one over the other. I said something about being in the military and needing to use military facilities, although there were none nearby. Then, from somewhere deep within, I heard myself saying, "Send her where she'll get the best care. It doesn't matter which hospital it is. I want her to have the best care possible. That's what's important."

It was my voice saying those words, but it certainly wasn't my thought, because I was incapable of thinking clearly at that point. I would realize later that it was Spirit prompting my words and guiding my actions even then.

Given the opportunity to decide, the doctor said he would transfer Deirdre to the University of Kansas Medical Center (UKMC) in Kansas City, Kansas. In his opinion, it was the best possible place for her. They not only had a pediatric intensive care unit, but were nationally known for their research and treatment of Reye's syndrome. He told us that it was fortunate that we were nearby so progressive a hospital and that we had been so observant and gotten Deirdre into treatment so quickly. Judging by the tests our family doctor had run only hours earlier, there was no evidence of Reye's syndrome at that time. He was hopeful that the quick diagnosis and treatment would work to Deirdre's benefit.

The few steps back to the examination room were some of the longest I have ever taken. I felt feverish and my pulse was racing, my heart pounding. All movement seemed blurred and the bright lights of the emergency room swirled around me. Standing near the exam room door, I called to Tino and told him what the doctor had said. I could see from his reaction that he knew all too well the seriousness of our daughter's condition. He suggested that I call some people from our study group and let them know what was happening.

Tino went back to Deirdre's bedside and a nurse directed me to a telephone. I called our friend, Brenda, explaining the situation to her through tear-filled words. I can't recall my exact conversation, but I did ask her to pray and to call the other members of our study group "at a decent hour" and ask them to pray as well. Then I hung up and rejoined Tino at Deirdre's bedside.

The medical staff was making the necessary arrangements to transfer Deirdre to UKMC. They expected it would take about two hours. When I tried to hold her hand, she tried to bite me. Tino and I watched helplessly as our daughter lay there, twisting and turning, thrashing about, biting, and emitting that shrill, high-pitched shriek. We would later learn that the agitation, the shrieking, the biting, and the "superhuman" strength we had witnessed were all characteristic behaviors of Reye's syndrome.

Each time I heard that piercing shriek it penetrated deep into my very bones. I knew it was having the same effect on Tino. I kept thinking that this couldn't possibly be happening, that this was a bad dream from which I would awaken. My once safe world had been suddenly thrown off course, and I felt as though I was plummeting uncontrollably through the depths of space. All faculties of thought and logic were lost to me, as if frozen in time.

Tino suggested that I call Brenda again and ask her to join us at the hospital. It was rapidly becoming apparent that we needed someone with us. Her husband Brad answered my second call. He told me that Brenda had already called everyone in our study group and was on her way to the hospital. She had realized the severity of the situation and hadn't wasted any time taking action.

I was standing at the nurses' station signing release forms when Brenda arrived. She told me that when she first arrived, she hadn't seen anyone and was unsure of where to go. Then she heard a strange cry echoing through the corridor and recognized it as Deirdre's. She followed the cries until she found me. As we talked, I realized that just having her there seemed to make me feel better. Tino felt the same way. We had someone to rely on, someone who could think clearly when we could not. We were no longer alone.

Brenda is an extremely psychic or sensitive individual, and one of her many gifts is the ability to "pick up" information that is not always evident to the five physical senses. After spending some time with Deirdre, she agreed that her spirit was no longer in her body, but where or why she had gone, she didn't know. Her soul was still connected to her body by the "silver cord" which is severed only at death, and that meant she could return. Knowing I was worried by her constant screaming, Brenda tried to reassure me that not being in her body, Deirdre wasn't feeling any pain. We were seeing her physical self, not her real spiritual self. This was small comfort, but it was comfort nevertheless.

Barely more than two hours after our admission to Shawnee Mission Medical Center, they were ready to transport Deirdre to UKMC. Looking back, I am still amazed at the speed and efficiency with which they examined Deirdre and came to the correct diagnosis. In such cases, every minute is critical, and the quicker the diagnosis, the quicker the treatment, and hence a better chance of recovery. By the time the ambulance had arrived, we had decided that Tino would ride with Deirdre in the ambulance, while Brenda drove me to our house so that I could pick up some things we would need.

While waiting for the ambulance, one nurse came up to me and asked if I would call her and let her know how

Deirdre was doing. She said that she had a daughter near that age and told me that she would be praying for Deirdre's recovery.

When the ambulance arrived, the nurses briefed its attendants as to Deirdre's agitated behavior, but despite these warnings they insisted they could handle her without a problem. Tino was directed to sit in front with the driver. It wouldn't be long, however, before the attendant riding in back with Deirdre would call out for the driver to stop.

"Send the father back here," he shouted. "I can't hold her down."

Tino spent the remainder of the trip struggling along with the attendant to hold Deirdre and keep her from climbing off the gurney.

Doubts and Fears

I stood and watched as the ambulance disappeared into the darkness of the early morning, feeling as though my life had disappeared into the darkness along with it. Fear, panic, and a sense of dread so intense I cannot even begin to put it into words took hold of me. I was aware of little else.

It was a only a short drive back to our home, but time had lost all perspective. Arriving at the house, I fumbled with the door lock. As I entered, I felt an eerie silence, a still and heavy feeling hanging in the air. The once joyous atmosphere of our home had vanished, replaced by an oppressive aura of dread.

As I walked through the house, I saw constant reminders of Deirdre's presence. The many drafts of her science paper were neatly stacked on the dining room table. Toys and clothes were strewn about, and I wondered with remorse why I had ever scolded her for not picking them up. If she came back, I would never scold her again. *If* she came back. I choked on the thought. Walking up the stairs to the bedroom, my feet felt like lead weights. Were these the same stairs I had so joyfully climbed two days ago to tell my daughter the success of her science project? Everywhere I turned I saw reminders of her. Tears began to flow as I wondered out loud if she would ever come back. How could I possibly return to this house without her? There were so many memories, so many reminders of her brief life with us.

I don't know what I would have done if Brenda hadn't been there. She gently coaxed me away from these dark thoughts and reminded me that there was no room for negative thinking. Deirdre would be coming back. We had to believe that; we could not lose hope. Everything would work out fine. Positive thinking, she admonished me. We had to focus on the positive.

Clearing my thoughts, I gathered together the things I had come for. First was "Softie," a blanket Deirdre's grandmother Jessie had given to her when she was born. There wasn't much left of Softie now, and we kept "her" in a pillowcase, so "she" wouldn't waste away into nothing. I then found Donald Duck, Deirdre's favorite stuffed toy. Donald had always been her favorite character. She could never understand why so many people seemed to prefer "that rodent mouse" to the "cuddly duck." It became quite a joke within our family. Deirdre never went to sleep without these two, and her stay in the hospital was not going to be any different. I also took a small, quilted blanket that had been made by Deirdre's Aunt Mary.

Returning downstairs, I found my address book. Then it was time to leave. I turned off the lights and locked the door, not knowing when I would return. As the garage door closed, I felt as if it were closing down on my world. Would it ever be the same again, I wondered. The car pulled out of the driveway and we headed for the hospital.

MAZE OF FEAR

As Brenda drove through the deserted streets, I began to talk idly, verbalizing anything that came to mind. I continued on for some time before I realized what I was doing. I had done the same thing years before when I learned of my father's death. I had been thousands of miles from home when I received the unexpected news. As I awaited the plane which would take me home to his funeral, I talked endlessly to a friend, recounting stories going back to my childhood. Fortunately, my friend understood that this was my way of dealing with grief. Now years later, with my daughter's life in danger, I was exhibiting the same behavior. I couldn't help but wonder if this meant that she, too, was going to die.

UKMC was a huge complex with many buildings. Unable to find the emergency room, we parked and entered what appeared to be the main building. We found ourselves in a deserted section of the hospital and passed through empty corridors and offices. We wandered anxiously from hallway to hallway, going up one stairway and down another, getting more and more lost in the process. A feeling of panic was beginning to take hold of me. My daughter was lying somewhere in this hospital and I couldn't find her. I was lost in a maze! It shouldn't be this hard to find the emergency room. I felt as if I were trapped in a nightmare from which there was no escape.

After what seemed an eternity, Brenda and I crossed paths with a maintenance worker who directed us to the main lobby. At last, I thought, we would be able to get directions. To our dismay, however, the information desk was closed and the main lobby was deserted. Looking around, Brenda found a map diagram and we headed in the general direction of the emergency room. I felt like shouting with joy when we finally arrived. Our frustrations continued, however, for no one there had any information about

Deirdre. There hadn't been an admission in the last two hours, and no one knew anything about a ten-year-old girl with Reye's syndrome. When an attendant smugly asked us if we were sure we were at the right hospital, my initial impulse was to reach over and grab him by the throat. I was at the breaking point! It seemed as if the universe was throwing up stumbling blocks all around.

Fortunately, a nurse intervened at this point and suggested that we check with the pediatric intensive care unit (ICU). It was possible that Deirdre had been admitted there. Following her directions, we made our way to the second floor and found the pediatric ICU. As we approached the waiting room, I saw Tino, quietly outlined in the darkness. I had to catch my breath and calm down before I could tell him of our difficulties. When I finished, he told us that Deirdre had been admitted directly to the pediatric ICU and was being examined. She was undergoing more tests, and a doctor would talk to us as soon as the results were available.

By now it was approximately 5:00 a.m. and due to the early morning hour, the lights were dimmed. In the darkness I could make out the forms of a young couple sleeping on cots set up on the opposite side of the room. Another woman lay sleeping on a couch covered with blankets. In addition to several sofas and a good number of chairs, I made out a rather large, round table, a television set, and a coffee maker. I remember thinking that the chairs and sofas seemed comfortable and that at least we had a decent place to wait.

This waiting room was reserved exclusively for families of children in the pediatric ICU, and many parents spent the night in close proximity to their children.

My thoughts were suddenly interrupted by the echo of a high-pitched shriek. I knew it was Deirdre's. She was so near and yet so far away. Her physical body lay in the next room, while the medical team worked desperately to save it. But where was my daughter really? I knew with certainty that the soul is eternal and that those separated by death meet again on a spiritual plane. I wasn't willing, however, to be parted from her this soon. We had only been together ten short years, and I had planned on many more than that. There was so much yet to do, so much yet to share. She had to recover. I couldn't consider any other possibility.

AN INSIDIOUS DISEASE

A short time later, we were called into the ICU to meet with the resident on duty. He confirmed that their tests did indicate Reye's syndrome, and he gave us some general information on the disease. Reye's is a viral disease, although the actual cause is unknown. It appears to develop following a case of influenza, upper respiratory infection, or chicken pox. In some cases, aspirin may be a triggering factor, but in other cases it is not. It is not known how the virus works, only that its effects can be observed. And although it primarily attacks the brain and liver, there is little or no evidence of the virus in these organs. It is characterized by fat accumulation in liver cells causing liver failure, and swelling of brain tissue which can lead to brain damage. The brain swelling is considered the most serious aspect of the disease and is the most difficult symptom to treat. Reye's is a leading killer of children under sixteen, with a mortality rate of 60%. There is no known cure, only a course of treatment that has proven successful in some cases.

Factors working in Deirdre's favor were her age and the fact that she had been admitted to the hospital at a very early onset of the disease. Success of treatment was related to how quickly the blood chemistry could be stabilized. The doctors also thought that it was a good sign that she was still responding to pain, as evidenced by her continued agitation.

The resident informed us that the head of pediatric neurology would be in shortly and after reviewing the case would talk further with us. It was this department that had spearheaded their research and treatment on Reye's syndrome. We could continue to visit Deirdre in the ICU as often as we liked, and we would be notified if there were any significant developments.

With nothing more to do at the moment but wait for further word from the doctors, we took time to notify our families. These phone calls were very difficult to make, for there was no easy way to break the news. The fear and sorrow in your own voice betrays you, and your listener knows that something is wrong before you can even deliver your message.

Although several of our closest relatives wanted to fly to Kansas to join us, Tino and I thought it best if they stayed at their homes. The stress and strain of a hospital vigil is a heavy burden and, although their presence was welcomed, we knew there was little they could do here. Their prayers would be just as effective from where they were. Prayer, we knew, knows no distance.

A DIM PROGNOSIS

By late morning, the head of pediatric neurology, Dr. Chaves, arrived. He had conducted a thorough examination and reviewed all test results. As the doctor in charge of the case, he reviewed the findings with us.

He repeated much of the same information the other doctor had given us regarding Reye's syndrome. Although he was fairly certain it was Reye's, he wanted to do a few more tests to rule out the possibility of other diseases with similar symptoms, such as meningitis and encephalitis. The high ammonia content of the urine combined with the low sugar level seemed to indicate that Reye's syndrome was the correct diagnosis, but he wanted to eliminate any other possibility. Treatment had already begun, and more specific modes of treatment would begin shortly. Since the cause and mechanism of the disease were unknown, treatment consisted of methods designed to alleviate the symptoms of the disease.

First, they were going to put Deirdre on a respirator, in order to ventilate her and help her expel fluid more quickly. Strong diuretics would be administered to help flush excess fluids out of the system. If symptoms persisted, they would begin treatment with corticosteroids designed to reduce brain swelling. Arterial catheters would be inserted to control various elements of her blood chemistry. The doctor's most immediate concern was the shrieking and agitation that Deirdre continued to show. This high state of excitement was causing the cranial pressure to increase. He was going to sedate her in order to restrict her movements. Finally, he informed us, they needed permission to perform minor surgery—to insert a cranial probe to monitor pressure in the brain. They would drill a small hole into the skull, insert the probe, and attach it to her head with a bolt.

I asked him how long we would have to wait before we saw some change in Deirdre's condition. He advised us that it normally took twenty-four hours to resolve such cases. Within that time, the patient either took a turn for the worse or began to recover. Either way, we could expect a change within twenty-four hours.

Tino and I consented to any procedure the medical team deemed necessary. Medical doctors, we believe, are instruments or extensions of God's healing power. Deirdre had the best medical technology available at her disposal and we welcomed its use to the fullest extent.

Prior to the surgery, Tino and I went to see Deirdre to explain to her what was about to happen. As I held her hand and stroked her head, I had the sudden realization that my sister, Darcie Callahan, who lived in Boston, must join us; something from within was telling me that she had to be here. At the same moment in which I was telling Tino about this feeling, Darcie was calling the hospital and speaking with Brenda. She had the same feeling as well and was in the process of making plans to leave Boston. She was calling to let us know she needed someone to pick her up at the airport when her flight arrived. As on so many other occasions in our lives, my sister and I were thinking in unison, our thoughts meeting in the realm of the universal mind. I went back to Deirdre's bedside and told her that her aunt would be with us soon. Then they came to take her to surgery.

Following the surgery, Deirdre lay quietly, unresponsive to any stimuli. I held her hand and stroked her head, relieved that she was no longer agitated. I knew that she was sedated, but was uncertain what this total lack of responsiveness meant.

I watched my daughter, my beautiful child, lying supine and unresponsive, her body violated by tubes and instruments. A respirator tube was thrust down her throat to control her breathing, while i.v.'s, carrying nutrients to her system, pierced deeply into veins in both arms. What disturbed me the most, however, was the loathsome "bolt" that they had drilled into her foreskull. Its cold, ugly metal protruded out of her delicate forehead and served as a constant reminder of the fluid pressure building up in her brain. I will never forget how I felt at that moment, and although Tino didn't say anything, I knew he shared the same feelings of despair and helplessness that I was experiencing.

It wasn't long before Dr. Chaves returned to tell us that they had completed their tests and were 99% certain it was Reye's syndrome. Her brain activity indicated that she was now "comatose." He then made a strange statement about the outcome of such cases. He said that it was their (the medical team's) experience that these cases were in God's hands. He said that he sometimes felt that for all their efforts, God had *already* determined the outcome of the case long before they even saw the child. All their procedures, he said, did nothing more than fill time until the final decision, life or death, was revealed. He told us that if we believed in God, now was the time to pray.

I remember thinking at the time that this was an odd statement for a doctor to make. Normally the doctor tries to convince you of the validity and importance of his procedures. Yet here, this doctor was basically telling us that the outcome of this case lay in God's hands and that there was nothing he could do to change that. Was this his way of telling us that her case was hopeless? Or, perhaps, was Spirit speaking through him, using him to reassure us that God was indeed watching over our daughter? I had to believe that the latter explanation was correct.

Fellow Travelers

Throughout the day other members of our study group had come to join us in our vigil. Sharon was the first to arrive, shortly after 8:00 a.m. She lived nearby and had been unable to go back to sleep after Brenda's phone call. She had lain awake, staring at the ceiling, thinking to herself that this couldn't really be happening. This was the kind of thing that only happened to other people, not to someone she knew and loved. After prayer and meditation, she got dressed and made her way to the hospital. This was no time to be alone.

The next to arrive were Dot and Bill. They, too, had been up praying, meditating, and calling other people within the A.R.E. Their phone calls had reached out to many people and, unbeknownst to us, a spontaneous, unplanned prayer network was beginning to form across several states.

By afternoon, Jeanne and her husband Rick had arrived. They lived in Lawrence, Kansas, and the hospital was a good hour's drive away. Yet despite their busy schedules, they had cancelled their plans to come and be with us. Joye had also called, wanting to join us at the hospital, but we thought it best if she stay at home and do her prayer work from there. Joye was very empathic and susceptible to strong emotions, such as those encountered in a hospital setting. There was no need to subject her to such a strain.

And so, our study group came together as a family to offer love and support in a time of crisis. We would make this journey together.

Body, Mind, and Spirit: All Healing Is One

The long hours of sitting in the waiting room that first day gave us ample opportunity to talk and consider the events of the night before, hoping to make sense of what had happened. The initial reactions of shock and panic were beginning to wear off, replaced by fear and helplessness. We knew it was necessary to work through these negative emotions. The early hours of our hospital vigil were, therefore, spent in discussions of our spiritual beliefs and a reexamination of what they meant.

Many metaphysical traditions teach that each individual or entity is actually a triune existing on three levels at once: physical, mental, and spiritual. The physical body manifests in the earth plane in material form or matter. It is but a temporary house for the soul. The mind is an active force or energy which is the controlling and building force of all we create in the physical. The soul is the creative life force which permeates the cells of mind and body. It is a companion in Spirit with the Creative Force or God and is our *real* self.

Disease occurs when one or more aspects of the individual is out of balance with its intended purpose. The purpose of all healing should be to bring the body, the mind, and the soul back into attunement with the Creative Force. The instruments of healing are many and can take any form. Edgar Cayce expressed this idea by pointing out that the instrument of healing can be preventive medicine, a curative drug, a skilled surgeon's knife, a positive thought, or an earnest prayer. Each has the ability to cure the body of physical ills when correctly applied. And though the instruments may vary, the source of all healing is the same. It is the one universal Spirit or God.

Medicine for the Body. Modern-day "allopathic" medicine is an intellectually oriented, analytical system which explains disease in terms of physical cause and effect. A mechanistic system, it does not accept what it cannot see, test, or verify. It seeks to treat disease by using agents that produce physical effects different from those of the disease being treated. As Dr. Chaves himself told us, they could not treat the disease because its origin was unknown. They could only treat the symptoms manifested by the disease through medications designed to counter these effects.

We viewed the medical treatment that Deirdre was receiving as a necessary extension of God's healing power. Its main purpose was to cure her body of disease and restore it to a healthy condition on the physical level. The doctors and nurses were using every means known to modern science to achieve this end. Although we accepted these efforts as vitally necessary, we knew they did not address the issues of mind and spirit.

The Mind-Body Connection. In recent years, there has been a quiet revolution under way in terms of how we understand the healing process. The medical profession is paying increasing attention to the ways in which the consciousness (mind) and body interact. Physicians, psychologists, and other researchers are coming to accept that a person's mental condition does have a direct effect on the immune system. Medical students are now being taught to treat the whole person, rather than just the disease. It is now accepted that certain diseases can be controlled not only through drugs but by changes in diet, exercise, and mental discipline. Cancer therapies have even gone as far as to include creative visualization, the practice of laughter, and self-hypnosis as part of their regimen.

The medical profession is also beginning to recognize the

importance of cultural differences and religious traditions in the healing process. Studies indicate that persons from non-Western cultures recover faster and more completely when allowed to practice certain cultural traditions. Many hospitals in the southwestern United States, for example, no longer object when a Native American patient requests a visit from the tribal medicine man as an adjunct to his or her medical treatment. Religious practices, such as prayer circles at the bedside, are also beginning to gain a wider tolerance. While the mind-body approach is a step forward from a purely mechanistic view of healing, it does not address the role of the spirit.

The Spiritual Dimension. As stated above, our real self is the soul, which is housed by the physical body while it sojourns on the earth plane. It is possible, at times, for the soul to temporarily leave the body and travel through the spiritual realm. During these journeys, the vital "silver cord," visible in psychic realms, remains attached so that the soul may return. Accounts of astral travel or projection are instances of this phenomena. Edgar Cayce discussed a similar process when he described how he obtained information during his psychic readings. He felt himself rise from his body and slowly travel along a path of light as he passed through various nonphysical environs. By continuing to follow the light, he came to a place of brilliant white where he entered a temple containing the akashic records, the records that comprise the history of each soul's existence. After accessing the required record and retrieving the information asked of him while he was in trance, he would then return to his body.

This phenomenon of the soul leaving the body occurs frequently during times of severe illness and has become known as the "near-death experience." Raymond A. Moody, M.D., is a leading researcher in this field. His work was continued and expanded upon by Melvin Morse, M.D., who conducted scientific studies of near-death experiences of children.[1] His research, published in the American Medical Association's pediatric journal, *American Journal of Diseases of Children,* indicated that such experiences occur only during cardiac arrest or in cases of deep coma.

Most near-death experiences are characterized by common themes, such as an encounter with a source of light, feelings of peace and happiness, contact with dead relatives or "angelic" beings, and a conscious choice as to whether to return. The uncanny ability to recall, in vivid detail, events which occurred around them while at the threshold of death is also a common phenomenon of the near-death experience.

The details patients describe, such as physical descriptions of the doctors and nurses, colors and positions of instruments, and the intricate details of medical procedures performed, can be verified later by those who were present. They also have the ability to recall, often verbatim, discussions which occurred in the emergency room, ICU, or even among people in the waiting room. Such detailed recall would not be possible unless the person actually witnessed the events.

Although the medical profession is still skeptical about the validity of near-death experiences, it is beginning to acknowledge that comatose patients, for whatever reason, may be much more aware than previously thought. Doctors are beginning to realize the importance of communication with comatose or dying patients. Based on the belief that a comatose patient *is* aware, negative comments are avoided, for they can have a detrimental effect while positive comments are encouraged as an aid to recovery.

DECISION POINT

As our discussions with our study group friends continued that first day, one thing was clear. We were at a decision point. We could choose to resign ourselves to the severity of the situation or we could continue to hope for a miracle. At that point, accepting the situation seemed like giving up, and we were not willing to do that. We had to keep on fighting, as long as there was a chance of recovery.

Somehow, during the long hours of that first day, it became clear to us that a miracle was not only possible, but was a reasonable course of action. Everything we had learned—from the Cayce readings to the *Course in Miracles* to the principles taught by Unity to the very words of Jesus Christ Himself—told us that miracles are possible. Jesus had repeatedly assured us that all that He did, we could do also: " . . . and greater works than these shall [you] do" . . . (John 14:12) It was time to take His words at face value and apply them as best we could. It was time to put our beliefs into action.

Positive Visualization. First, we had to maintain an attitude of positive thinking. The process of positive thinking or creative visualization[2] has long been taught in many quarters. It is based on the knowledge that everything in the physical universe is made up of energy, and the fact that form (physical manifestation) always follows idea (thought). The energy of each thought, feeling, or object vibrates at its own distinct frequency, and since energy is magnetic, it will attract that of a similar nature. Once energy is generated, a physical manifestation will follow, whether or not direct physical action is taken to bring it about. The mere act of holding the thought or energy in mind will begin the process of creating that form. Consider the artist who first holds the thought of the masterpiece he or she will paint long before the brush ever touches the canvas, or the composer who first imagines the melodic tones used to create a symphony. The process is the same. Knowing that thought (energy) can create things (physical conditions), we had to look beyond the physical illusion of the situation and affirm that Deirdre's bodily condition could be changed. By concentrating our thoughts on healing and recovery, we hoped to work with the natural principles that govern the workings of our universe and help bring healing into manifestation. We could not afford to entertain the idea of a negative outcome, for that would bring a negative result to fruition. Only positive thoughts would create positive results.

Communication. The research on near-death experiences showed us that our thoughts and actions could be perceived by Deirdre even though she was comatose. Realizing that communication with her was a vital element of recovery, we decided to take turns visiting her to reinforce thoughts of healing as much as possible. As we sat by her still body, we would talk out loud, hold her hand, and stroke her hair. We talked about our love for her, our prayers for her, and how much we wanted her to return to us. We asked her to help us understand why she had left and asked her to let us know what we could do to hasten her recovery. We affirmed that she could and would recover.

Just as Deirdre was aware of our words and actions, she was also aware of our thoughts and prayers. For prayer, as spiritual energy, is not bound by humanmade laws of time and space. Knowing that we could direct our thoughts and prayers to her, we often prayed while at her bedside. We balanced bedside vigils with periods of private meditation and prayer. The environment at UKMC was conducive to this type of bedside vigil. A progressive hospital, it is very supportive of the concept of treatment of the whole person. The administration personnel do not enforce outdated restrictive ideas about time and duration of visits, nor do they restrict visitors to immediate family members. No one ever questioned our efforts, and as long as we did not interfere with their work, the nursing staff actually encouraged us to spend as much time with Deirdre as possible. As the hours turned into days, they taught us how to perform simple procedures, such as changing the i.v. bag, clearing out the respirator tube, and rolling Deirdre while her bed sheets were being changed. Perhaps this tolerant attitude

was the reason we had been led to this particular hospital.
Momentary Setback. Our bedside vigils continued into
the night, as Brenda, Darcie, Tino, and I alternated efforts to
sleep with bedside visits to Deirdre. I was aware that Darcie
had been quite restless and assumed that she was spending
time in the ICU. Unable to sleep, I went to join her. As I
passed by the restroom located immediately inside the ICU
doors, I heard a cry. It sounded like someone saying, "Help
me." I entered the bathroom and found Darcie sitting on
the floor, too weak to stand. She had been vomiting for the
last several hours, but hadn't said anything earlier because
she didn't want to be a bother.

I quickly found a nurse and asked for help. She told me
that Darcie would have to go to the emergency room for
treatment and helped me find a wheelchair. I woke up Tino
and explained the situation. He would take her to the emergency room. As they disappeared down the hallway, I sat in
disbelief, staring into the darkness. Evidently, Darcie had
been more severely affected by her niece's illness than anyone had realized.

She remained in emergency for several hours. When she
was discharged early that morning, Sharon took her to our
house where she stayed for the next three days. Her debilitated condition made it impossible for her to stay at the
hospital. At the time it was difficult to understand this development, although we would later understand the reasons behind it. We did know that we could not let this
momentary setback dampen our spirits or shake our faith.
We had to believe that divine order was at work and continue on the path we had started.

FIRST STEPS

We did not realize it at the time, but our discussions and
actions in those early hours of the first day were the first
steps of a spiritual journey and were to set the direction our

path would take. Like children learning to walk, we were taking our first hesitant steps. Learning to walk is not easy, but it is a natural part of the growth process. It is a milestone in a child's development that will change his or her interaction with the world from that point on. The child, however, has no way of knowing how those first steps will change his or her life. We, like the child, had no way of knowing the significance of our actions, nor did we realize that they would change our perception of the world forever.

✱ ✱ ✱

You ought not to attempt to cure the eyes without the head, or the head without the body, so neither ought you attempt to cure the body without the soul. —Plato

2

Prayer in Action

Prayer is a rising up and a drawing near to God, in Mind, and in Heart, and in Spirit. —Alexander Whyte

A Call for Prayer

As morning dawned on the second day of our hospital vigil, there was a renewed feeling of hope and expectation. The doctor had told us to expect a change in Deirdre's condition within twenty-four hours, and we were confident that the change would be for the better. Those members of our study group who had gone home for the night returned early the next morning. There was some initial dismay as they learned about Darcie taking ill. We tried, however, to put this momentary setback in perspective and focus our attention on maintaining a positive attitude. Then we anxiously awaited news that Deirdre's condition had improved.

The early hours of that morning brought two visitors. The first was Chaplain Shaft, the staff chaplain from my navy command. He talked to us a while and then went to pray at Deirdre's bedside. When he was finished, he encouraged us not to lose faith, but to continue to hope and pray that she would recover. Our second visitor was the hospital's Protestant staff chaplain, Reverend Jennie Malewski. She, too, talked with us and prayed at Deirdre's bedside. She was pleased to learn that we believed in the reality of miracles, for she said that she had seen more than one miraculous recovery during her years as a hospital chaplain. Their words of encouragement were very welcome, for although we were well aware of the wonder-working power of prayer, it was good to have this belief reinforced by others.

The importance of prayer was known to us from the outset of our hospital vigil. The first and only request we had of friends and relatives was to join us in prayer. We also knew that the power of prayer increases as the number of people involved in the prayer effort increases. This was one reason we had contacted two prayer groups—the Glad Helpers and Silent Unity. The Glad Helpers Prayer Healing Group is affiliated with the A.R.E. and consists of A.R.E. members who pray for people who request and seek healing for themselves. Operating continuously since 1931, this prayer group meets weekly at the A.R.E. headquarters in Virginia Beach, Virginia. The members also pray daily, by name, for those who have asked to be put on the prayer list, and they maintain a prayer chain for emergency situations. The prayer list is updated weekly, compiled monthly, and sent out to over 2,000 prayer-partners throughout the world who join in prayer on a daily basis.

Silent Unity is a prayer ministry of the Unity School of Christianity in Unity Village, Missouri. Approximately 100 individuals answer telephones and pray with people of all faiths in four languages. Over 100 additional people respond to nearly two million written prayer requests each year. In addition to five daily prayer meetings, there is always at least one person praying in a continuous, twenty-four-hour vigil of prayer. This vigil has been in operation for over a century. After individuals seeking prayer contact Silent Unity, they receive a letter and a printed prayer by mail.

With the aid of these two groups and the prayers of our family and friends, we felt we had a solid base of support for our prayer effort. The prayer network would expand and grow in size and intensity as the days progressed and would come to play a vital role in our healing efforts on the journey that lay ahead. We had no way of knowing, however, the extent to which this phenomenon would spread.

THE UNIVERSAL LAW OF PRAYER

Our belief in the power of prayer was based on the premise that prayer is a universal law which is in continual operation. As such, it is possible to work in harmony with its principles and, by aligning oneself with these universal forces, bring about a desired result. By working in compliance with the law, you can bring order out of chaos, and all things become possible.

The Creative Power of Prayer. There are as many definitions of prayer as there are people who pray. One definition, as given in the Cayce readings, is:

"Prayer is the concerted effort of the physical consciousness to become attuned to the consciousness of the Creator, either collectively or individually."[1]

Prayer is an attempt to attune oneself with the spiritual forces of the universe. It is an attempt to bring the earthly consciousness or mind into oneness with the Creative

Forces. Once oneness or alignment is achieved, prayer energy can be used as a creative, active force which can make things occur and actually change physical conditions.

On the universal or spirit level, prayer is the key which allows us to regain our birthright as co-creators with God. It enables us to tap into the Universal Consciousness and, once in attunement, use that force as an active agent of change. On the mental or soul level, prayer raises our sights to the divine level and enables us to visualize conditions as they can be when we work in harmony with the universe. Prayer permits us to see that the only true reality is that which God has created. On the physical or earthly level, prayer enables us to see that the negative conditions which appear in our lives are but temporary, human-made illusions which can be changed. The spiritual energy of prayer can be focused on physical conditions to effect positive change.

It is necessary to understand that our attunement with the Creative Forces is influenced by the attitudes we hold toward ourselves and others, our feelings, our emotions, and our state of mind. If we harbor doubt, negative feelings, or resentment, then our ability to attune to the universal forces will be adversely affected, and thus the outcome of our prayer. Our purpose must be selfless; a desire for self-gain or self-aggrandizement will influence our ability to attune. Prayer must be more than idle words or thought without substance. It must be backed by faith, emotion, and expectation. We must also learn to align ourselves with the Universal Will, rather than with our own will, because it knows better than we what is truly in the interest of our highest good.

We must, in essence, try to become one with the Creative Forces of the universe, acknowledge that this force is all good, all knowing, and wants only the best for us. We must understand that this process has already begun and is in fact being fulfilled as we pray. This is what Cayce referred to as "effective" prayer; he went on to say that through it you can accomplish more than through all earthly power and might.[2]

The Healing Power of Prayer. Science teaches that all mass or matter is really energy. Light, thought, and ideas are energy also. Science further teaches that energy can manifest as a force. Prayer, as a form of thought, is best visualized as a form of pure white light which can be focused as a force and released to a specific destination. Upon reaching its destination, this energy has the ability to impact the vibrational pattern of its recipient, thus creating new conditions. This vibrational impact first occurs on the unconscious or superconscious level before changes manifest in the physical. Healing prayer is thus the application of thought or energy which, through attunement with the universal forces, affects positive changes in a physical condition, resulting in healing.

Prayer for Another. The concept of praying for another or "intercession" is practiced in many religions. Roman Catholics, for example, often invoke intercession by the saints or the Virgin Mary. A Cayce reading addressed the issue thus:

"Who may make intercession? They that have within their consciousness a channel to the throne of grace, that there may be given into the mind and activities of the soul of this entity those influences that may bring the changes in the experience of this body."[3]

When prayer is directed to another, the healing itself is actually accomplished by the recipient, who must be willing to accept and draw upon the healing energy being received. The law of free will ensures that this is so. The healing energy of a prayer offered by another can help the recipient to attune with the universal forces if he or she so chooses.

Group Prayer. Just as light is magnified by the addition of candles to a darkened room, so, too, is the power of prayer magnified when done in unison. Jesus Christ spoke of this when He said, "Wherever two or more of you are gathered in My Name, so too am I in the midst of you." (Matthew 18:20) A Cayce reading explained it thus, "In unison of purpose is their strength. In the prayer of those that would aid comes strength *with* that unison of purpose in Him."[4]

In other words, as the number of people joining in prayer for a common purpose increases, the resulting power of that prayer is dramatically increased. As the thought or prayer energy generated by the people involved is released, it creates a type of synergistic effect in which intensity of the energy grows exponentially rather than proportionally. The energy of prayers joining in unison is of a greater force than the combined individual energies of the prayers.

Testing the Power of Prayer

To some people, the explanation of the creative, healing action of prayer may seem like a fanciful flight of imagination. They demand proof; they demand a concrete explanation. Just because the reasons behind a phenomenon cannot be explained does not mean that it does not exist. Many of the recent discoveries in quantum physics regarding particle behavior defy explanation. The use of cloud chambers to study subatomic particles shows that these particles mysteriously appear out of a void, only to disappear once again. How this happens is not known, yet it does happen. The bumblebee is aerodynamically incapable of flight and yet it flies. It defies explanation, but the results are evident. Do we ignore the truth simply because we cannot understand it, or do we accept its validity based upon the evidence of results? Various studies have been conducted to determine the power of prayer on effecting certain outcomes. The results of these experiments prove repeatedly that prayer helps, prayer works, and prayer can effect change.

Dr. Randolph Byrd. At the University of California Medical School, San Francisco, Dr. Byrd conducted a study[5] on the effectiveness of prayer. The results, published in the *Southern Medical Journal* in July 1988, provided conclusive evidence that applied prayer did enhance the recovery of patients.

The study was conducted on 393 patients in the coronary care unit who had either experienced a heart attack or were suspected of once having had one. These patients were divided into two groups. There were no statistical differences between the two groups and each received identical care. The only difference was that one group received prayer and the other did not. It was a double-blind test in that neither the staff nor patients were aware of which group was receiving prayer. The first names of the group members receiving prayer and a sketch of their physical conditions were given to various organized prayer groups throughout the United States. The prayer groups were then asked to pray for these individuals, although they were not told how or when to pray.

The results showed that those who received prayer were five times less likely to need antibiotics and three times less likely to need diuretics. This group also had significantly fewer instances of cardiac arrest, less incidence of pneumonia, and none required endotracheal intubation. At the time of publication, this study raised many questions within the medical establishment.

Spindrift Studies. The Spindrift Organization in Salem, Oregon, has conducted numerous studies over the years regarding the ability of prayer to affect the behavior of simple biological systems, such as seed germination or the metabolic rate of yeast cultures. These studies repeatedly show that prayer does have a definite effect on such systems.

A secondary finding of these studies is the evidence that nondirected prayer is more effective than prayer which seeks a specific outcome. Although both methods have the ability to affect processes, the results indicate that nondirected prayer has a more powerful or measurable effect.

Some speculate that this may be related to a concept known as divine order, which states that there is an inherent rightness in the universe that will manifest when permitted. The law of prayer responds to the principle of divine order, which ensures that the highest good of all concerned is manifested.

APPLYING EFFECTIVE PRAYER

Convinced of the validity of the belief that prayer could directly affect Deirdre's physical condition and bring about healing, we made a conscious attempt to apply effective prayer. In effective prayer, God is not Someone to pray *to*, but a depth of awareness and energy to pray *from*. Such prayer does not involve praying *to* God, but rather praying *from* the consciousness *of* God, projecting a spiritual power in a transcendental flow to heal and harmonize conditions.[6] More than just mere words or wishful thinking, effective prayer, sometimes called scientific prayer, follows a specific methodology, although the steps vary slightly from method to method. The following guidelines for effective prayer are taken from suggestions given by Edgar Cayce, Charles Fillmore, and the *Course in Miracles:*

1. Acknowledge the oneness of God and know that this Creative Force is the source of everything in the universe.

2. Seek attunement as the real goal of prayer; make your will one in accord with divine will.

3. Release unforgiving thoughts, resentments, or any ill will you may harbor.

4. Know that prayer must be from within and must be sincere or selfless. Prayer for the purpose of self-aggrandizement is self-defeating.

5. Release all thoughts of the outer physical world; acknowledge negative conditions as illusion.

6. Acknowledge that once you have set the pattern, the Creative Forces will handle the details.

7. Pray with an attitude of expectancy; know that the uni-

verse is answering your prayer even as you ask it.

8. Release the outcome to God, knowing that divine order will seek the result which is for the highest good of all concerned.

This type of effective prayer has great potential if correctly applied. It has the ability to harness thought energy, direct it to a specific destination, and bring about changes in physical conditions. It has, in effect, the ability to create miracles.

We added the practice of effective prayer to our efforts at positive visualization and our continued attempts to communicate with Deirdre. As we prayed, we concentrated on surrounding her with the pure white light of healing and visualized her as healthy, whole, and perfect.

PNEUMONIA SETS IN

It was late morning on the second day after we brought Deirdre to the hospital when a nurse told Tino and I that Dr. Chaves wanted to speak with us. Surely, we thought, he would have some good news. Surely he would tell us that there had been an improvement in her condition. As we met him in the corridor inside the pediatric ICU, the look on his face was solemn as he told us that there had been a change, but that it had not been for the better. Their most recent examination showed that pneumonia was setting in, a disease which could severely strain her already weakened condition. *Pneumonia!* Upon hearing this news, I felt as if my heart had leapt into my throat only to fall and plummet to the floor. Another disease was attacking my daughter. Lost in thought, I barely heard Dr. Chaves describe the treatment they would have to begin in order to control the effects of the pneumonia. Again, we gave permission for the medical team to pursue the course of treatment they deemed necessary.

Returning to the waiting room, I felt anxious and frightened. This news filled me with dread. I could not control the tears which streamed down my face. Tino was silent. The news hit everyone else in much the same way, for this turn of events was totally unexpected. Things were not going as anticipated or hoped for. Instead, the opposite seemed to be occurring, as Deirdre's physical condition deteriorated. Fear gripped my heart once more, and I knew the others were feeling it as well. What had gone wrong?

As I stood crying alone in the hallway, out of the corner of my eye I saw my commanding officer walking down the hall toward me. His arrival forced me to pull myself together. When I informed him about our situation, he was incredulous. He evidently had no idea of the severity of the situation. He had not expected to encounter a life-and-death situation and was completely unprepared. When I related Dr. Chaves's comment about the outcome being in God's hands, he stared at me in disbelief. I knew from my experiences with the captain that he was a man who was very much focused on the material world, with little concern for the spiritual. He was simply unable to comprehend how a man of science could make such a statement.

As we talked, I realized that the captain was present because he, too, was a part of our learning experience. I felt compelled to explain some of our beliefs to him. As I talked, I asked Spirit to guide my words. He sat and listened without saying a word, and I was sure he was questioning the state of my sanity. When I finished, he made some comments about the high quality of the hospital and gave me the standard offer of support. It was obvious that he was uncomfortable and wanted to leave. He had made the obligatory visit required of a commanding officer and I was certain that, having fulfilled that duty, he would not return. He would prove me wrong.

After his departure, I realized that by explaining my beliefs to him, I had, in effect, reaffirmed them for myself. The old adage that one learns best by teaching others is certainly true. It is often those times when we think we are the teacher, that we are, in truth, the student.

An Enemy Called Doubt

The development of pneumonia was the subject of much discussion that afternoon. Things were not going as we had planned, prayed for, or anticipated, and we pondered the reasons for this turn of events. Perhaps, we conjectured, this was the darkness before the dawn. Whatever was happening, God was certainly testing us. Dot hit it precisely when she said that we were all being "stretched" far beyond our previous limits. Such stretching, we knew, though painful, is often an opportunity for growth. As Oliver Wendell Holmes once said:

> "Man's mind stretched to a new idea never goes back to its original dimensions."[7]

It is one thing, however, to intellectually accept the premise that "all things work together for good" and acknowledge the idea of all situations as presenting learning experiences, but it is quite another matter to believe this from the heart when a child's life is hanging in the balance. We all had doubts that day, doubts about the validity of what we were doing, doubts about the effectiveness of our prayers, and doubts about the possibility of a miracle. And even though we knew we were supposed to look at this not as a crisis, but as a stepping-stone to greater growth, it was no easy task, for the doubts we felt were at times overwhelming.

Recalling Cayce's words of "Why worry when ye may pray?"[8] we sought to occupy ourselves with prayer and other activity as a means of keeping our doubts at bay. It took a combined, concentrated effort on the part of all of us to deal with these thoughts. Whenever one of us wavered and felt doubt creeping in, the others would rally round and lift that person's spirits.

Our faith had been shaken, yes, but it was not shattered. If we let our faith be destroyed this easily, there mustn't have been much substance to it to begin with. Through tears, hugs, and anguish, we bonded together to reaffirm our faith and the belief that a miracle could still happen. The road had become more difficult, but it was not yet impassable. By now we were committed to the path we had chosen and there was no turning back.

MANY BELIEFS: ONE PURPOSE

Our attempts to overcome our doubts and move beyond the obstacle in our path prompted us to take further action, action which would have the effect of expanding the prayer network. That afternoon, we again called family and friends to update them on the situation, and calls also went out to people we had not previously notified. Our purpose was to increase the number of individuals in our prayer circle and thereby increase the power of healing prayer being directed to Deirdre.

As we made these calls, we discovered that many of our relatives, friends, and co-workers had given Deirdre's name to their local churches that Sunday morning. Congregations in several states had joined in prayer. Thanks to the efforts of my shipmates, word spread quickly through the navy community and many fellow service members joined in the prayer effort. Dot and Bill made calls to other A.R.E. members and study groups they had been associated with, asking for their prayers as well as any information or guidance they could provide. Tino's family had notified still others, and many within the Native American community were actively at work.

Darcie had already set in motion a network among numerous Wiccan circles in the New England states. Wicca is a nature-oriented religion that views the Divine as both God and Goddess. Its members refer to themselves as witches and maintain that the religion is not satanic. It involves magical practices related to seasonal changes and the need to heal the earth and its inhabitants. In addition to the traditional prayer groups, many Wiccans would also be performing healing rituals on Deirdre's behalf.

It would take several days for us to realize the true extent of this prayer network. It stretched from Maine through New England to New York; to Virginia and down the eastern seaboard to Georgia; across the Midwest, including Missouri, Illinois, Kansas, and Nebraska to Colorado; through the southwestern states of New Mexico and Arizona to California; up to Washington State, into Canada, and across the Pacific to Hawaii! It consisted of people from varied religious backgrounds: Protestant denominations such as Lutherans and Southern Baptists, Roman Catholics, Jews, Wiccans and ceremonial magicians (particularly the Order of Ganymede), Buddhists, Pentecostal Christians, Unity congregations, Native American groups, and Rosicrucians. Some prayed to God the Father, others to the Goddess. Some prayed to Jehovah, the God of Abraham, while others prayed to Jesus the Christ. Still others invoked the name of the Holy Spirit, the Universal Mind, or the Great Spirit of their ancestors. Some raised their voices to the Virgin Mary and the communion of saints. Requests for prayer spread by word of mouth, from individual to individual, from group to group, and from congregation to congregation. Though they called the Universal Spirit by different names, they were able to lay aside surface differences and direct their prayers, meditations, and healing rituals toward the common goal of healing a little girl.

This was perhaps the most unusual aspect of our experience. The vast variety of religious groups which became involved in the prayer effort was truly remarkable. Across the country, individuals and groups, most of whom we did not know, were actively directing their prayers toward healing our daughter. Although their theological differences were significant, their purpose was the same. All came to offer their own unique and special kind of help, uniting in the spirit of love. The many hues of the rainbow of the human spirit had joined together to form a beautiful, brilliant white light.

No Answer in Sight

Our prayers and bedside vigils continued throughout what seemed like an endless day, as one hour slowly merged into another. As I sat by Deirdre's bedside, I realized that I had become so accustomed to the repetitive "ka-huh-shoo-ook" sound of the respirator's calculated rhythm that I barely noticed its noisy operation. I looked with dismay at the monitors I had learned to read, monitors which tracked so many of my daughter's bodily functions. One measured her heart beat and another measured her pulse. A large monitor tracked the amount of fluid pressure in her brain. This was perhaps the one I watched most frequently for it read out as a simple number. With normal brain pressure being in the fifteen to eighteen range, I cringed each time I saw the monitor registering a number in the high twenties, sometimes topping out at thirty. Her body was being so viciously attacked that I wondered with fear how long she could endure the ravages of this disease.

By early evening, there was still no perceptible change in Deirdre's condition. The Reye's virus was still affecting her liver functions and the brain swelling had not subsided. The medical team was experimenting with different drugs in the hopes of finding those that would be most effective. Other than the pneumonia, there had been no significant changes in her condition. It seemed as if we were suspended in a state of "limbo." The hours dragged on and on. At times I would sit and watch the clock tick off second by second, minute by minute. It was the interminable waiting that seemed to be the most draining.

As evening approached, Dr. Chaves came to tell us that

he was leaving for the day and would return the next morning. I reminded him that he had said we would see a change within twenty-four hours and yet nothing seemed to be happening. He responded that although that time frame was true in most cases, it sometimes took longer, say forty-eight hours, before the turning point was evident. Deirdre's case was evidently progressing in this manner.

His words left us with an empty feeling that night. I wondered why he hadn't told us this is the first place. I had expected a change that day, and now I would have to endure another night and wait another day. I feared that Deirdre was not responding as they had hoped and the doctors were stalling for time. Two long days had passed, days which had taken a heavy toll on everyone, and I wondered how much longer we could endure this waiting. I was already so tired, so fatigued. I wasn't sure I would have the strength and resolve to endure much longer.

LAUGHTER AS A FORM OF PRAYER

The somber atmosphere that night was alleviated by the arrival of Tom Abate. Tom was a chief petty officer with whom I had worked for over two years. He had no particular interest in metaphysics, but I suspected that he and I had been comrades-in-arms more than once. Tom knew Tino and Deirdre very well. In fact, he and Deirdre had a special kind of relationship: whenever they were together, they played and teased one another as if they were long, lost friends. The study group knew Tom from the many stories I had told about him and our "adventures" in the navy. He had a family of his own, including a son and daughter near Deirdre's age, and he had nearly lost his youngest daughter during childbirth two years earlier; he could well empathize with our situation.

The previous evening he had come alone, but tonight he was accompanied by his wife Debbie. His appearance was again like a gift from heaven, for his mere presence lightened our burden, if only for a few hours. For Tom had the unique ability to make us laugh.

The value of laughter cannot be underestimated. There is a valid reason why it has been called "the best medicine" for both body and soul. It alleviates anxiety, relieves stress, reduces pain, and lifts depression. Charles Fillmore, the co-founder of Unity, called laughter "one of the most direct and effective shatterers of fear."[9]

Studies on the phenomenon of laughter have shown that it has the ability to heal the body by inducing the release of beneficial hormones and chemicals from the endocrine glands. Laughter causes the pituitary gland to release pain-killing endorphins and enkephalins, and the adrenals to release epinephrine, norepinephrine, and dopamine, all of which fight pain and inflammation. Laughter has also been shown to improve blood flow and reduce blood pressure. When engaged in laughter, the creative, right side of the brain is more active.

On a deeper soul level, laughter sends a subtle message to our subconscious mind. Through laughter our problems can be seen in a different light, our actions seem more positive, and our results more attainable. Laughter has the unique ability to help us see through the illusions of the physical world and comprehend the true reality of the spiritual world. It does not change our situation, but it does change us. And since laughter has the ability to effect change on both a physical and a spiritual level, it can be thought of as a form of prayer.

When Tom arrived, it was as if a bright light came on in the waiting room. As he told his jokes and stories, everything suddenly seemed brighter. He held our attention and made us laugh. We laughed so hard that most of us had tears running down our checks. If anyone had seen our group, they would never have guessed that we were keeping watch over a child fighting for her life only a few yards away. And if they had known, they would have thought us insane.

Yet for us, this laughter was a form of healing prayer. In addition to the physiological effects if must have had, it affected us on the spiritual level as well. For a few brief moments, we were able to cast aside our fears and believe that yes, everything was going to be okay. Tom's jovial presence was one of those unexpected gifts encountered along the mountain path, a gift for which we will be forever grateful.

ANGELS AFOOT

Tom and Debbie were not our only visitors that Sunday evening. Tino's friend Pat and her husband, Bill DuChane, also joined us. Pat was just learning about metaphysical phenomena and listened intently to us as we described what we were trying to do. Then, as the evening was drawing to a close, Reverend Mary Omwake arrived. Mary was the pastor of the Unity Church of Overland Park, which Deirdre and I were attending, and the instructor of the "Unity Basics" course in which Brenda, Sharon, and I were enrolled. I really didn't know Mary very well at the time, having only met her casually at Sunday services and class, but for some reason I felt a need to see her. I couldn't escape the feeling that Mary was supposed to be a part of this experience. We had left numerous messages for her over the course of the last two days, but had received no answer. I realized that she would be busy with Sunday services and commitments, but I continued to voice my concern that we needed to see her.

When she arrived, we learned that she had not received any of our messages. She had come because she received a phone call a little more than an hour earlier, begging her to go to the hospital. We would later discover that it was Brad who had made the call, for he had realized on his own how desperately I wanted to see Mary.

It would be several weeks, however, before we would

learn the complete details surrounding this call. It seemed that Mary had had a particularly difficult day, which had left her physically and emotionally exhausted. She had just gone to bed when the phone rang and a highly agitated person was frantically begging her to come to the hospital. When she expressed reluctance due to the late hour and offered to come the next day, the person offered to *pay* her for her time. The offer of payment made her feel so guilty that she dragged herself out of bed and forced herself to get dressed, even though her heart was not in it. As she drove to the hospital she cried and asked God for the strength to get through this visit. She had expected to find a distraught and grieving family that would draw upon her for strength and support. Instead, she said, she found a family so focused on love, support, and faith that we actually raised her up and made her feel better.

Mary spent some time visiting with us and meeting everyone. Then she asked to see Deirdre, alone. She stayed quite some time before returning to the waiting room. When she returned, she asked us if we realized that our daughter was an "ancient soul." Tino and I answered that we did. She felt that Deirdre had left her body to seek information regarding certain questions, information that was not available to her except by this method, information that she felt was worth risking her life to obtain. It seemed that Deirdre was in the middle of a "coaching session," asking many questions and receiving information from many sources. Mary felt that the Master Himself was holding Deirdre as they sat in the midst of a hearty discussion. Mary did not know what information Deirdre was seeking, but she knew that Deirdre felt that this had been her only option. Mary then told us that she sensed the presence of angels, many angels, in both the pediatric ICU and in the waiting room. It appeared that we were receiving help and support from many levels.

Mary's words gave us renewed hope and encouragement, for we knew she was a most intuitive person, a profound healer, and very much in tune with the oneness of the Creative Forces. We wanted to believe her words were true, and our belief system told us that this was possible. The fact that Mary was able to discern so much information and validate some of our own perceptions was a great comfort. She stayed a while longer and would later tell us that we had made her feel so much better that she was reluctant to leave. Our journey was going to prove to be a learning experience for her as well.

Mary's comment on the presence of angels was not the first such reference made that evening. Tom had related to us that the previous night he had an unusual experience while driving home. He had left the hospital for the long drive back to his home in Missouri. As he proceeded along the freeway, a strange thing happened. He suddenly saw an angel. He said only that this angel was so beautiful that it brought tears to his eyes. He was aware of nothing else. Then as suddenly as it had appeared, the angel was gone, and he found himself across town in Missouri, a good thirty miles away. He could not remember driving through the city.

The fact that Tom shared this experience with us showed us the impact it had on him. He had no prior interest in this sort of thing and was concerned that we were going to think he was crazy or worse yet, making it up. When we assured him that we did believe him, he seemed relieved. The fact that two totally different people spoke of angels that night was no coincidence to us. We took it to be proof of the fact that angels were no doubt afoot and watching over us all. Indeed, over the next few days numerous visitors would make similar observations. We also came to realize that angels do not always have to be ethereal, heavenly creatures. Tom and Mary were proof of that.

WALKING ON

The late hours of that evening were perhaps even more difficult for us than the night before. Dot and Bill had brought two cots for sleeping, and we had plenty of pillows and blankets, but that didn't help us rest any easier. The day's events weighed heavily on us and had left us more confused than ever. Our high hopes and expectations of the morning had been dashed by the development of pneumonia and Deirdre's continued unresponsiveness to treatment. Sleep came in short spurts, interrupted by fitful dreams and the need to keep watch over Deirdre.

At this point, we were very much like toddlers learning to walk. The joy and excitement of those first steps are often followed by confusion and doubt as the child trips and falls. We, too, had taken those first hesitant steps, only to find ourselves stumbling over a rock in the road. The toddler, however, overlooks this momentary setback and is quick to pull him/herself back up to try again. It is only by repeating this process over and over that the child will eventually learn to walk. Like that child, we had to pull ourselves back to our feet, step over the rock, and continue on.

As our journey unfolded, there would be more rocks and boulders, more "stumbling blocks." The pneumonia would pale in comparison with what lay ahead. Yet once committed to the path, there was no turning back. Each obstacle had to be turned into a stepping-stone, for our daughter's life depended on us proceeding forward. The road was long and winding and at times it wasn't clear where it led. We had to trust that Spirit would guide us.

❋ ❋ ❋

Prayer travels more strongly when said in unison.
—Petronius

3

Step by Step: Guidance Through Dreams and Meditation

Concerning all acts of initiative and creation, there is one elementary truth—that the moment one definitely commits oneself, then Providence moves, too.
—Johann Wolfgang von Goethe

WE awoke Monday morning to a flurry of activity we had not previously experienced during the weekend. At 7:00 a.m. a hospital volunteer had turned on the lights in the pediatric IUC waiting room, broke open a box of doughnuts, and began to make coffee. Members of a cleaning crew began to vacuum and tidy up. Even the menu in the hospital cafeteria was different that morning, with a greater variety of food items available. The number of people hurrying about to and fro made for a more hectic atmosphere than the quiet pace we had grown accustomed to over the weekend.

We had been eating all of our meals in the hospital cafeteria, dividing into groups and taking turns so that someone would remain in the waiting room at all times. I had actually come to look forward to our mealtimes; it was the only break many of us had from the interminable hours of waiting. I had just returned from breakfast and was waiting for the doctors and nurses to finish their morning routine. Each morning Deirdre was examined by a medical team, had an EEG, and a chest x-ray. She was also bathed and turned, and her linen changed. We made it a point to be as unobtrusive with our bedside vigil as possible and always stayed out of the way when medical personnel were working with Deirdre. I believe the nurses appreciated our consideration as much as we appreciated their tolerant attitude toward us.

As we waited for the medical team to finish with their morning routine, we chatted with the two other families who shared the waiting room with us during the past two days. Janet was the grandmother of five-year-old Matthew, who had cerebral palsy and also suffered from a seizure disorder. This was not the first time he had been hospitalized with severe convulsions, and the doctors had also told them that there was very little hope that Matthew would survive this latest episode. His family was from out of town and had several other children to care for, so his parents were unable to spend much time at the hospital. To help ease their burden, Matthew's grandmother had offered to stay. She spent most of the day in the waiting room and slept at a nearby Ronald McDonald House at night.

The other family that shared the waiting room with us included the parents and grandmother of a three-month-old baby girl, Morgan. Morgan had a seizure disorder of some sort that caused her to convulse whenever she was picked up. It's hard to imagine what it's like to be unable to hold your baby. Her parents were very young, not quite past their teen years, and yet they were bearing up remarkably well under this most heavy burden.

We had added both Matthew and Morgan to our prayers, based partly on something Mary had said the night before. She had told us that Deirdre was very worried about Matthew and that we needed to pray for him as well. After discussing it further, Dot recommended that we add a third child, because she remembered the Cayce readings advising people to pray in threes. It was obvious to us that Morgan should be the third child in what I termed our "prayer triad."

We were strangers brought together by grievous circumstance, suddenly sharing a common, though unwelcomed bond. I think it helped all of us to talk and share our feelings, because it made us realize that we were not alone. There were others who understood our fear and pain.

Stumbling Blocks Abound

It usually took several hours for the medical team to complete Deirdre's examination, evaluate the tests, and discuss their findings. As he had on the previous day, Dr. Chaves spoke with us to bring us up to date on Deirdre's condition. Although she had a stable night, it appeared that she had developed a fever, indicating an infection of some sort. The problem was that they weren't able to identify the source of the infection. She would have to be treated with additional antibiotics as well as medicine to reduce the fever. There was one positive note to this development: the fever indicated that her immune system was still capable of mounting an attack against the infection. In other words, she was still fighting.

The elation I felt after hearing that small ray of hope was quickly deflated, however, as Dr. Chaves cautioned us that

Deirdre's brain pressure was still at a dangerously high level. In fact, they were not sure how much brain damage might have already occurred. They had administered one medication after another, all to no avail. Each drug seemed to work for a short time and then cease to have any effect. They were running out of things to try and had only one remaining course of action to pursue.

This course of treatment involved administering phenobarbital, a barbiturate drug which would have the effect of depressing the brain functions. The rationale behind this was to alleviate the internal stress and agitation which were causing the continued build-up of fluid in the brain, the accumulation of ammonia in the liver, and elevated temperature and blood pressure. In effect, the doctors would be shutting down her bodily functions in an effort to give her body a rest from fighting the consequences of the disease. After an eight-hour period, they would wean her from the medication and hope that physical functions would return to a more normal, less agitated level. They had scheduled a brain-imaging test for later that afternoon, a test that would measure the blood flow in her brain. This would give them a better indication of possible brain damage.

Following our consultation with Dr. Chaves, Tino and I returned to the waiting room and relayed this newest information to our friends. Once again, our hopes and expectations had gone unfulfilled as Deirdre's physical condition continued to deteriorate. Our prayers did not seem to have any effect. Each small ray of hope seemed to be followed by an even greater disappointment. It was like being on a roller coaster. The good news which sent our spirits soaring was quickly followed by bad news that sent us rocketing downward. By now our nerves were strained beyond a level we had ever thought possible, and it was becoming increasingly difficult to see this as a learning situation. In fact, it was nearly impossible.

Returning to Deirdre's bedside, I found my mind filled

with thoughts of regret and remorse. Was there something I should have done but didn't? Was there something I could have done differently? Had I pushed her too hard on her science project? Had I paid enough attention when she first said she wasn't feeling well? Why hadn't I been more sympathetic when she complained of stomach pain? I had told her that there were times when we had to be strong and just take the pain and see it through. I had even chided her for complaining too much. The guilt I felt was tremendous, and the tears stung my cheeks as I regretted ever saying those words. Now I was telling her how sorry I was for saying them and that I knew she was fighting the battle of her life, as she valiantly struggled against the disease ravaging her body.

In addition to the respirator, i.v.'s, and cranial bolt, other tubes had been inserted into her inner thighs to carry drugs to her body, while still other tubes carried fluids out of her body. At one point, I counted nine separate tube lines protruding into or out of her body. My once carefree, joyful child was engaged in a battle for her very life, and I stood by powerless to help. All I could do was pray and wait for something to happen. I had never felt such desperation, such utter helplessness.

I didn't know how much longer I would be able to cling to the belief that a miracle could still happen. And yet I was afraid to give up hope. I felt that if I gave up hope, it would be paramount to accepting the inevitability of Deirdre's death. And if I gave up, how could I expect her to go on fighting? I could not, I would not give up on my daughter.

And neither would Tino, nor any of the others. I knew we were all having similar thoughts. Tino, Brenda, Sharon, Dot, Bill, Jeanne, Joye, and Darcie, still at our house, were struggling with their own personal demons just as I was. Tino was particularly upset because he felt there must have been something more he could have done to prevent this. He had made several attempts to help Deirdre in the hours just prior to the onset of Reye's and was feeling a sense of guilt and failure because his efforts had not worked. It was a constant struggle to fight off the doubts and fears that haunted us all. It was taking all our combined strength and resolve to adhere to our convictions and maintain faith that a miracle was still possible. Yet not one of us was willing to give up.

SEEKING ANSWERS

As we struggled with our doubts and fears, we kept thinking that there must be something more we could do. If we only understood why this was happening, we might have a better idea as to how to proceed. All of our conversations seemed to keep coming back to the one question which had as yet gone unanswered—why? Besides our concern for Deirdre, this thought was foremost in our minds.

We knew the "how" of the physical disease, but we had not uncovered the "why." We knew that disease is more than a physical phenomenon with physical causes; all disease has its roots in the realm of thought and ideas. Like any physical manifestation, this disease must have had its inception in the mental realm of thought. Mary had said that Deirdre had left to "obtain information." But other than that we had nothing specific to go on. What had prompted Deirdre to embark upon this dangerous path? Were there clues or warning signs we had missed? Deirdre's illness had taken everyone by surprise, and we were all stymied by its sudden onset. Many metaphysical traditions teach that there are no accidents and that every circumstance has motive and purpose, but we had as yet been unable to understand what these might be.

We hoped that if we understood the underlying reasons, it might provide us with further guidance as to what we should do, what action—if any—we should take. We also thought it would help alleviate our fears, because fear often stems from the unknown. The more you understand something, the less you fear it.

We did have many questions concerning this issue, but we realized that the answers to these questions would not be found in the physical world of our five senses. The answers would have to come from the Universal Mind.

THE UNIVERSAL MIND

The concept of "The Universal Mind" or "collective consciousness" is centuries old and is found in many cultures. In Sanskrit it is called *Shakti* or *Chiti*. The Taoist sages referred to it as *Te*, the Jewish mystics called it *Shekinah*, and the ancient Greeks named it *Sophia* (wisdom). According to Indian saint Swami Muktananda, *"Chiti is . . . the only cause of creation, sustenance and dissolution of the universe . . . the prime cause of everything . . . She is all-pervading . . . Manifesting as the universe . . . there is nothing apart from Her . . . the One who is called cosmic consciousness."*[1]

The Universal Mind is based on the premise that all knowledge, thought, wisdom, ideas, and understanding exist as a collective which is independent of time and space. In other words, all that has been, is, or will be exists in an energy form which permeates the universe of physical space. It is much like the concept of "The Force" popularized by the *Star Wars* motion picture trilogy and readily accepted by millions of its fans. The Jedi master Obi-Wan-Kenobi explained "The Force" to Luke Skywalker as 'an energy field created by all living things. It surrounds us and penetrates us. It binds the galaxy together."[2] As an anthropologist, I know that the characters in *Star Wars* represent mythological archetypes with which people of all traditions can identify. Perhaps the popularity of these movies may also be due, in some part, to the fact that people *do* know, on a subconscious level, that the Universal Mind or Force is real.

The Universal Mind is everywhere present and works in and through every circumstance and condition in our lives.

Because it encompasses all knowledge, the Universal Mind expresses itself as divine order or divine will in that it always brings about that which is in the best interest of our highest good or spiritual development. Problems arise in our understanding of this because that which is truly in the best interest of our spiritual development may cause temporary pain on the physical level, and it is the immediate pain that we perceive and react to. The other side of the coin is that something which appears to be in our best interest may in reality be a detriment to our highest spiritual good. The popular country-western entertainer Garth Brooks captured this sentiment with his song "I Thank God for Unanswered Prayers."

Since we, as individuals, do not have all information at our disposal, we do not know the total picture. We react only to the present moment. The Universal Mind, however, does possess all knowledge and, therefore, knows the complete picture. We must, then, trust that divine order knows what is best for us and align ourselves with divine will so that our highest good can be made manifest.

As spiritual beings, we are a part of this universal force. When we enter the earth plane and assume a physical body, however, a cloud or "veil" separates our earthly, conscious mind from direct access to the Universal Mind. It is a condition necessitated by the density of the physical body, a condition of physical laws that we accept when we return to the earth. God, however, does not wish us to be separated from His Universal Mind, so He devised a means by which we can access it, even while in physical form. And while these methods do take practice, they can be learned and developed by anyone.

Access to information in the Universal Mind can be gained through many channels. The key to each proven method, however, involves releasing the constraints of the conscious mind and passing through to the subconscious/superconscious levels of the mind. When the earthly consciousness is released, our soul self can penetrate the "veil" of separation and thus access the information stored in the Universal Mind. This is what Christ meant when He said "the Holy Spirit . . . will teach you all things and bring all things to your remembrance." (John 14:26 NKJV) As we consciously practice and develop our ability to use these methods, we learn to gain more conscious access to unconscious information which can benefit us.

Attunement to the Universal Mind does not come by seeking guidance from outside sources, but rather by looking *within* the soul self. Remember, "The Force" runs in and through us, not around outside of us. The psalmist spoke of this when he said, "Be still and know that I am God." (Psalm 46:10 NKJV) We can all learn to turn our conscious mind to the Universal Mind or Spirit within. The most common avenues of access to the Universal Mind are dreams, meditation, and intuition. Dreams are perhaps the most common method of accessing the Universal Mind. One reason is that, whether intended or not, the dream state creates the effect of stilling the conscious mind so that the deeper levels of the mind can take hold. Dreams can, therefore, represent contact with spiritual forces and, when so focused, can provide information and guidance to the seeking soul. The importance of dream study has been recognized for thousands of years. The Bible itself contains numerous examples of dream analysis and recounts several instances of angels appearing in dreams to warn of impending danger. In the modern world, twentieth-century psychoanalysis revived the practice of dream study, and today it is a part of many recognized psychotherapies.

Meditation results in a state similar to the dream state except that it requires a conscious effort to set aside the physical self. According to the Edgar Cayce readings, meditation can be defined as an "*emptying* self of all that hinders the creative forces from rising along the natural channels of the physical man"[3] or the "attuning of the mental body and the physical body to its spiritual source."[4] By deliberately setting aside the conscious self, we allow expression of the spiritual self to come forward and through the spiritual self become open to information coming from the Universal Mind.

Intuition may be the least recognized method of obtaining information from the Universal Mind, but it is also one of the easiest to learn. It can best be described as a "hunch" or "feeling" one may have. It is the *"still small voice within"* (I Kings 19:12) which always speaks the truth. You have no need to question it for you somehow know that what it tells you is true.

Many people may be familiar with this concept through the popular television show *Magnum, P.I.*, which used it frequently during its nine-year run. In many episodes, the hero Magnum referred to "my little voice." When he followed his little voice, things turned out right, but when he ignored his little voice, things went very wrong. As the years progressed, Magnum came to trust his little voice more and more, even to the point of following it when it contradicted the "obvious physical evidence." In all those episodes, Magnum's little voice never once led him astray. I've often wondered if the writers of this show knew they were introducing millions of people to the idea of intuitive ability.

Intuitive ability varies greatly from person to person. Those who continually ignore their hunches will find them occurring less and less frequently. Intuition, like a muscle, will atrophy if not regularly exercised. On the other hand, those who acknowledge their hunches and—more important—*act* upon them will find them increasing in frequency. This brings us to an important corollary of accessing information in the Universal Mind. It is not enough just to *know* the information, you must *act* on it as well. "Knowledge, understanding, is using, then, that thou hast in hand," say the Cayce readings. "Do that thou knowest to do *today* . . . Then tomorrow will be shown thee for that day!"[5] It is only when we use the knowledge that we have at hand and apply the information we know that we are given further information that allows us to proceed to the next step.

Those of us in our study group family were at varying degrees of proficiency with dream study, meditation, and the practice of intuition. We had been actively seeking guidance through these channels since Deirdre first became ill. We had even asked others to keep attuned and be receptive to any information about Deirdre that might come their way. Yet, other than Mary's intuitive belief that Deirdre was seeking information in some celestial coaching session, we had received no other insight, no other guidance. We were as much in the dark as when we had started. When would we see a ray of light? When would we be allowed to understand the "why" of our situation and be shown where to go from here?

We had done what we were supposed to do. We had applied what we knew to do. We had utilized effective prayer, we had worked with positive visualization, and we had practiced openly communicating with Deirdre. As far as I was concerned, tomorrow had come and then come again, yet still no guidance was forthcoming. We had not been shown the next step.

Then, quite without warning, just as an abrupt shift in the wind causes a ship to veer off course, our path up the mountain took an unforeseen turn as we suddenly began to receive information, often from the most unexpected sources. Once the door was opened, information began to flow like a stream of rushing water which, suddenly breaking through the dam, gains in strength and intensity as it cascades over the rocks below. At last we were gaining access to the information we so desperately sought. The issue now would be whether we were ready to accept the answers.

SIGN OF THE RAINBOW

Joye was the first person to have a dream that provided some information, even though it was of a general rather than specific nature. Joye called that morning to tell of a dream she had the previous night. She had dreamed that she was watching a violent storm at sea. The wind was blowing, waves were crashing, thunder was booming, and lightning flashing. Then suddenly the wind died down, the seas calmed, and the storm disappeared. There on the horizon she saw the sun rise, and as it rose it was joined by a beautiful, vibrant rainbow. Then the dream ended. It was a short and simple dream, but she felt certain that it had to do with Deirdre.

After hearing about this dream, we all hoped it was a sign telling us that this turbulent episode would soon subside, and the sun would shine on us once again. The rainbow, we knew, could be a symbol of God's promises to us, and we hoped that it foretold a "happy ending."

PAST-LIFE ISSUES

The source of the most detailed information regarding the "why" of this experience would come from a woman who had never even met Deirdre. Jan Snyder was a friend and A.R.E. associate of Dot and Bill, who was well schooled in certain Native American traditions. Dot and Bill had asked for her help and, after learning of our plight, she entered a drumming trance at her home, during which she received a great deal of information.

During the trance, she learned that Deirdre had been feeling a strong influence from a past life,[6] a life which she had undertaken for the purpose of completing a specific mission. For reasons unknown, the companions who were to help her complete that mission were not available to assist her when the time came. She felt she had been deserted and "left all alone." She had decided to carry out the mission anyway, but it was too great of a burden for her to accomplish by herself and so she failed. It was possible that her death in that life was a direct result of her attempt to carry out this task alone. She had left that life with a great deal of fear—fear of being left alone, fear of pain, and fear of failure.

Deirdre had entered this life with a similar intent, to complete some main life purpose, and had agreed to and accepted that karma prior to entering the earth plane.[7] For some reason, Deirdre had begun to confuse this lifetime with the previous one when she had been unable to complete her life's purpose. The old fears of abandonment, pain, and failure had resurfaced, and she was questioning her ability to carry out her mission in this lifetime. She was afraid and confused, and did not know where to turn. She was, after all, just a ten-year-old girl, and although she was an ancient soul, she still filtered her experiences through the mind of a child. In an act of desperation, she had made a decision to seek information on the spiritual level and felt that the only way to do this was to leave her body and go directly to the source. She, therefore, had attracted a physical condition—Reye's syndrome—to her which would enable her to accomplish this.

None of this was done on a conscious level. It was not as if she had made a conscious decision to contract Reye's syndrome. Rather, these thoughts and fears had all occurred within the subconscious and superconscious levels of her mind. But because thoughts are things, her thought energy was able to affect physical matter and, in essence, create conditions conducive to the manifestation of a disease. There was no unjust God or impersonal universe imposing this upon my daughter at all. Deirdre had *chosen* this path. When Dot first conveyed Jan's information to us that Monday, we were somewhat stunned, and it took a while for us to digest its meaning. After some consideration, however, each of us had the feeling that it did make sense. It did seem to "ring true."

What was most surprising was that this vital information had come from someone who did not even know Deirdre.

As I pondered the significance of this revelation, my thoughts drifted back to the months of my pregnancy when I was first preparing for Deirdre's birth. I knew from the Cayce readings that a pregnancy is more than a physical birth; it is an opportunity to draw a living soul into the earth plane and allow it expression. I had followed Cayce's recommendations on ways to become a channel to draw the "proper" soul into the earth plane, and Tino and I frequently speculated as to what type of soul would choose us as parents.

When Deirdre was born, Tino and I, as do all parents, thought our child was special. Judging by Deirdre's behavior in the first few hours following birth, we felt she was one of those ancient souls who Cayce said return to earth with a full awareness of their purpose. For nearly three hours in the recovery room after delivery, Deirdre never cried, but turned her eyes first to Tino and then to me, holding each of our gazes for the longest time. Her large dark brown eyes scrutinized us with a piercing intensity. I had never seen a baby this calm, this self-assured. Even the nursing staff commented on her extraordinary behavior and her ability to "look right through you as if she knows what you're thinking." I have no doubt that she, as do many newborns, had the ability to look beyond the physical and see into the soul. As the years passed and Tino and I watched our daughter grow and mature, we often mused on what had brought us together as a family. We sometimes wondered what our life purposes might be. Jan's information seemed to confirm our belief that Deirdre did enter this life for a very specific reason, but this was certainly not the way we had expected to receive confirmation of that fact.

As we continued to discuss Jan's information, Bill brought

up another point for us to consider. In today's rapidly changing world, it was possible for conditions to change so quickly that the purpose for which a soul had originally entered could no longer be accomplished. He recalled that the readings said that some souls were given the option to review their situation and make a final determination as to whether they wanted to leave the earth plane or remain to continue on an alternate path. He felt that it was possible that Deirdre was in this position. She was being given the choice to stay or to pass on.

This realization filled me with an even greater fear. This was no longer a matter of trying to effect healing on the physical level. There were many forces at work here, many factors which we did not understand. Whether it was due to rapidly changing conditions or confusion from a past life, or both, one thing was becoming increasingly clear. Deirdre had left the earth plane to seek information that would help her decide if she would complete her original life mission or embark upon an alternate path, in this plane or another. She had a choice to make, and I was terrified as to what that choice could be.

FURTHER CONFIRMATION

When Mary came to visit again, I accompanied her to Deirdre's bedside. I watched as she stroked Deirdre's head and gently ran her hands over her limbs and body. I thought to myself that she had a "healer's touch." She stopped at the base of the skull and gently pressed her hands to Deirdre's neck. Then she moved to the liver area and touched that as well. Mary began to talk to Deirdre as we usually did. She began by telling her that she was loved and that she would never, ever be alone. She told her that promises made long ago were no longer binding. She did not have to do anything she did not want to do. She kept repeating that she was loved by many and would always have many people around her. As we prepared to leave, Mary told me that it would be helpful to picture Deirdre as a lamb, a little lamb that would always be loved and cared for.

Mary's words took me completely by surprise, because although I had not told her about Jan's revelation, her insights seemed to confirm and indeed coincide with the information Jan had received. I was excited and hopeful, because this could mean that the information was accurate.

I did not know Mary's beliefs on reincarnation at that time, because reincarnation is not a part of Unity doctrine, although some Unity members do accept it as a possibility. Yet something told me to tell Mary about the information we had received, and so I shared Jan's insights with her. It wasn't until much later that I would learn that the concept of reincarnation was fairly new to her. It had only been a few weeks earlier that Mary had somewhat reluctantly come to accept the idea of past lives as a possibility. My words had taken her by surprise, for I was providing her with validation of this belief, and she began to wonder why she had been drawn into this journey. At the time, however, she never gave any indication of surprise, and I never suspected the impact my words had on her.

The Turtle Call

We thought Jan to be an unexpected source of information, but the next call we would receive came from an even more unlikely source. On Tuesday morning, while Darcie was still at our house recovering from her own illness, she received a phone call from John, a friend who lived in New York. Receiving information from John may not have been too odd, because he had met Deirdre and had spent time with her when she was visiting her aunt in Boston. John, however, was not the one who had received the information. It had come through a friend of his who did not know us.

John had just received a call from Cheryl, one of the many people involved in the remarkable prayer network that Deirdre's illness had created. She had called because of a dream she had in which she was told that Deirdre was worried about a "turtle." She thought that perhaps this was a pet turtle or one of the "Teen-age Mutant Ninja Turtles" which were so popular at the time. In any case, the dream had been strong enough that she felt it necessary to call John and make sure he relayed the information to us.

News of this dream hit me like a jolt of lightning. Not only did it come from a total stranger, but I knew exactly what it meant. I knew exactly who the turtle was—it was *I*. The previous year I had been given information that the turtle was one of my "spirit animals" in the Native American tradition, and once I heard this I realized that it was true. I had started to collect turtle figurines and several of them decorated our house. Deirdre was not worried about a pet or a stuffed turtle. She was worried about me.

It was hard to believe that a stranger thousands of miles distant had received information about Deirdre. We had been receiving calls from people involved in the prayer network that we did not know, but they had all been of an inquisitive type, inquiring as to whether there had been any changes. The implications of this incident did not escape our attention. Even strangers separated from us by thousands of miles were receiving information about our situation! It was hard to comprehend just what was happening. The Creative Forces were most certainly working in strange and mysterious ways!

RAINBOW MEDITATION

The study group was quick to act upon this piece of information. They felt that if Deirdre was worried about me, it was necessary that I communicate with her and let her know that I was okay. The consensus was that meditation would be the best way to accomplish this. I was not particularly anxious to pursue this, because I did not feel I was as adept at meditation as several of the others were. Unlike some group members who meditated every day, I was more sporadic in my meditation periods, which ran in cycles. I knew, however, that it had to be done and so I agreed.

Fortunately, the hospital chaplain had arranged for our use of a consultation room as a place to pray and meditate. I entered the room by myself and prepared to enter the silence. I began by praying to Jesus Christ and the Holy Spirit, asking their protection and guidance. I asked that I be allowed to speak with my daughter so that she would hear what I had to say.

After some time, I must have entered a meditative state. Slowly, in my "mind's eye," an image began to take shape. I saw a foggy mist of some sort, which began to solidify into a screen, and I knew there was someone standing behind this screen. As the screen parted, I saw a young woman, perhaps nineteen or twenty years old. Although I did not recognize her physical appearance, I knew it was Deirdre. I began to "mentally" speak with her, telling her how much her father and I loved her and how much she meant to all of us. I told her how much we wanted her to return and reassured her that she would never be alone. Then I told her that I was all right, I would be okay. After all, I was a turtle, a survivor. The hard shell I had brought into this world had always protected me and, like the turtle who had survived millions of years of change on earth, I, too, would survive. Whatever decision she made, I would understand. I told her not to worry about me, but to take care of herself first. I also told her we believed it was still possible for her to return to us whole and healthy, if she wanted to do so.

Then without warning, the young woman began to glow with a brilliant white light. The light grew in size until it completely encompassed the young woman and she disappeared into the glow. The white light continued to expand

and then suddenly burst into a dazzling display of brilliant colors. Rainbow colors.

It was all I could do to keep from crying out. This rainbow light was the most beautiful thing I had ever seen. And I knew that at that moment I was seeing Deirdre's true self, her soul self. Still in meditation, I dropped to my knees, completely in awe. I was in the presence of a spiritual being. My daughter, I felt, was so much greater than I. But no, I understood that that was wrong. Then I realized that this was not only Deirdre's true self, but I was seeing the true essence of *what we all are!*

Words are inadequate to describe my thoughts and feelings. Time froze for me, and I truly believe that in that single brief moment, I was one with the Universal Mind. Still on my knees, I felt tears streaming down my face, and I thanked God for allowing me to see this. Then the rainbow light of colors began to fade and standing before me was Deirdre, my ten-year-old daughter. I thought she looked at me and then her image disappeared.

Still awestruck by the experience, I remained on my knees for some time. When I finally managed to get to my feet, I sat alone for a while, trying to understand what had just happened. Had I really experienced what I thought I did? Had I actually been allowed to see a glimpse of our true selves? Had I talked to Deirdre? Had she heard me?

I thought that perhaps the young woman I saw was Deirdre as she appeared in another lifetime, perhaps the life she was confusing with this one. I had seen my daughter as she was, as she truly is, and as she appears now. I could only hope that the fact she had returned to her present appearance was an indication that she would eventually return to us.

Still trembling from the emotion of this experience, I left the consultation room and returned to the waiting room. It was several more hours before I could share this meditation with anyone. I have never had such a profound meditation before or since. I truly believe that in my hour of need, the Holy Spirit took me by the hand and became my guide.

MOVING BEYOND THE DOUBT

At last, we had finally begun to receive the information we had so desperately sought. We now had answers as to the "why" of our situation, but we soon realized that these answers hadn't really helped us as we thought they would. They had given us understanding, but they had also raised a whole new set of questions. Motivational speaker, author, and business consultant Anthony Robbins's statement that "Questions set off a processional effect that has an impact beyond our imagination" [8] was certainly true in this instance. We had been so anxious to find out "why," and now that we had an answer, we did not like its ramifications. This new information had only given us more issues to consider, and as our confusion grew, so did our doubts.

It was as if the narrow path we had been walking suddenly led us around a corner revealing a beautiful meadow right there before us. At first we were anxious to enter the meadow because it afforded us a greater view. But as we moved onto the grass, a fog descended and we soon found ourselves losing all sense of direction. We no longer had a narrow path to follow, but were surrounded by ambiguous trails leading in obscure directions. We knew, however, that there had to be a sign or a light post to help guide us through, and we were determined to find it.

*   *   *

He who asks questions cannot avoid the answers.
—Cameroon proverb

4

Faith in Action

Faith is the daring of the soul to go farther than it can see. —William Newton Clarke

The Universal Law of Faith

THERE is one proven method that has for centuries repeatedly demonstrated its effectiveness in guiding people through the stormy sea of crises and helping them conquer the enemy of doubt. This method is centered around a belief in a Higher Power greater than ourselves, a spiritual power that is ready to help us at all times. Simply put, this method is faith, "the substance of things hoped for, the evidence of things not seen." (Hebrews 11:1) Faith enables us to look beyond the here and now and see things as they can be.

According to Cayce, faith is an attribute of the soul, an inner spiritual knowledge of the Creative Forces. It cannot be taught in a class or forced upon someone through persuasion. It can only be developed through acceptance, experience, and practice. When exercised, faith will increase in effectiveness. When denied, however, it will cease to exist.

Rather than being a passive quality, faith involves an active component which enables faith "energy" to be directed toward specific conditions to effect change. As Bruce McArthur explains in his book *Your Life: Why It Is the Way It Is and What You Can Do About It*, faith is "the ability to perceive that through the infinite power and wisdom of the Spirit within, working through the Universal Laws, nothing is impossible . . . The law of faith is: Whatever you ask in prayer, you will receive, if you have faith."[1]

Affirmations and Denials. One means of practicing the active component of faith involves the use of affirmations and denials. An affirmation is a positive statement about a condition or physical state, a positive assertion that a condition is so, even if the physical evidence is contradictory. A denial is a statement that denies or removes the power from a negative condition. It does not deny that the condition exists; it rather erases or dissolves our erroneous belief that the condition can control us.

Affirmations and denials are used in conjunction. Once the power of the negative condition has been denied, you affirm the condition you want to bring into existence. For example, in working with healing Deirdre, we did not deny that she was ill, because Reye's syndrome does exist as a fact in the material world. What we did deny was its ability to control or have power over her. We then affirmed that she was healed, whole, and healthy.

The consistent practice of using affirmations and denials

enables us to exercise an active faith. As we learn to deny negative conditions and replace them with a belief in positive conditions, we learn to use our thoughts to create and control our circumstances. We move toward reclaiming our birthright as co-creators with God and hence a closer realization of our oneness with the spiritual forces. Since the use of affirmations and denials teaches us that our thoughts can change our physical world, they are an important element of healing.

Faith and Healing. The exercise of faith, then, is that which enables us to acknowledge our birthright as co-creators with God. It empowers us to work in attunement with the spiritual energy of the Creative Forces and thus effect change in the physical world. Since faith can change conditions, it can be applied to help bring about healing through the God-Force. James Coyle Morgan, a Unity minister, put it thus, "There is no disease or malformation of the body that God power cannot heal when faith and expectation are strong enough." [2] The resultant healing is always for the highest good of the person concerned.

Scientific studies support the premise that creative imaging can affect the physical body. When the mind holds a clear image of a specific condition, the limbic system of the brain treats that image as a blueprint and sends a message to the hypothalamus to meet the specifications of that blueprint. The hypothalamus is the "regulator" gland, which directs bodily responses to correspond with the blueprint. In other words, when we create an image, our bodily processes are subconsciously directed toward attainment of that goal. The more the image is projected and the more emotion that accompanies it, the more effective is the physical result. This phenomenon is well known in the sports arena, and high-tech athletic training frequently includes the use of visualization techniques as a means of improving performance.

Maintaining faith in the face of adversity is not an easy

task, however, and it requires much more than the repetition of affirmations and denials. The doubts and fears which cloud emotions make it necessary to continually rely on a support system of some sort to sustain and reinforce our belief in the power of faith. We tend to look for proof, for solid evidence that faith can indeed bring about miracles. Some people find such proof in the inspirational stories of miracles past or from the direct support of others who provide comfort and encouragement in times of need.

BIBLE PROMISES

Several of us found ourselves relying upon the words and promises of Jesus the Christ for hope and comfort. The old familiar Gospel lessons and Sunday school stories teach us that miracles can indeed happen. The wealth of information found in Christ's parables and promises was not given us to be used as a history of what had happened. Rather, Christ's words indicate that He expected us to practice His teachings and apply them in practical ways in everyday life: ". . . the works that I do shall he do also; and greater works than these shall he do . . . " (John 14:12)

I personally found hope in the story of the Roman centurion whose servant had been healed by Christ from a distance simply because the centurion *believed.* (Matthew 8:13)

Each time I had doubts about our ability to effect healing, I came back to this story. I could even picture Jesus speaking to the centurion and seeing his servant rising from his bed as the healing took effect. If this had happened for the centurion, could it not happen for us?

Christ had made it very clear that through faith anything was possible. " . . . If ye have faith as a grain of mustard seed, ye shall say unto this mountain, Remove hence to yonder place; and it shall remove; and nothing shall be impossible unto you." (Matthew 17:20)

His teachings indicate that we, like Him, are co-creators with God, if we but realize our oneness with God and claim our birthright. Yet we need to remember that we are not the source of the healing, but rather God, Spirit, or the Creative Forces working in and through us. "... the Father that dwelleth in me, he doeth the works." (John 14:10) My family, friends, and I were now seeking to claim that birthright.

FIRST VISITORS

While inspirational literature is certainly a source of hope and comfort in times of crisis, by far the biggest uplift to our spirits came from the many people who rallied around us to provide support and encouragement. Monday morning marked the start of a steady procession of visitors that would last for days. Some of the people who came were friends, while others were people we had not met before, but had been made aware of our plight through the prayer network. They came from many walks of life, and the number and diversity of our frequent visitors became the subject of much comment and speculation.

The first visitors that morning included several of Tino's co-workers and friends—Pat, Carol, Dusty, and Myrna. They were all employed in the nursing profession and, after visiting Deirdre, were well aware of the seriousness of her condition. They offered their prayers and comfort and love. The doughnuts and muffins they brought for us were as welcomed as their prayers.

Monday also marked the day we notified Deirdre's school. As I spoke to Mrs. McKay, the school secretary, I could sense the shock she felt when I told her the news. Deirdre had always been a very outgoing child and was well known to many of the school staff. I know it was hard for them to comprehend that the happy-go-lucky child they had seen only a few days ago was lying in a coma fighting for life.

A short time after I called the school, I received a call back from Mrs. Kramer, the school nurse. She asked many questions about Deirdre's condition and then stated her intent to visit us. I told her it wasn't necessary and was quite surprised when she insisted on coming to the hospital. I was even more surprised when she came to visit Deirdre each day that week.

EVIDENCE OF MIRACLES

People continued to arrive throughout the day. Most were friends and co-workers from my navy command or the nursing home where Tino worked. The captain of my command came again, this time bringing his wife, and we discussed our beliefs further. All came to express their concern and support, and spent time visiting with us. They also brought food for us—baked goods, casseroles, fried chicken, sodas, and pie, along with paper plates and utensils. Someone even brought a cooler to keep the food fresh! By evening our corner of the waiting room resembled a well-provisioned campsite and was beginning to raise a few eyebrows among the hospital staff.

The love and support these people offered was invaluable, and each person made his or her own unique contribution to help us keep our hopes up and spirits high. There were three instances, however, that had a great impact upon us and provided us with actual evidence of the miracle-working power of faith.

Triumph over a Dark Prognosis. A story which demonstrated the power of prayer was told to us by Vonda, a civilian who worked with me at the navy command. Vonda had been plagued with her own health problems in the form of a back injury, and it was obvious that she was in pain when she came to visit. The fact that she cared enough to come despite her own pain meant a great deal. Vonda shared with us the story of her grandmother, who had been very ill and near death. The doctors had predicted that she would not survive the week. Her family also had great faith in the power of prayer and avidly put it into action. However, her grandmother not only recovered, but six years later was still leading a productive life. "Don't give up hope," Vonda admonished me. "I saw a miracle happen with my grandmother, and I know it can happen for you, too."

A Child Survives. The second story of inspiration came through a phone call from Deirdre's godmother, Pat, who was living in California at the time. During one of her calls she told me the story of her friend's young daughter who had also been hospitalized with a life-threatening illness. Her parents were told that she would not survive and yet, several days later, she made an amazing and unexplainable recovery. Again, further evidence that miracles can and do happen.

Cancer Conquered. Perhaps the most dramatic story we heard was an account given by Steve, a fellow navy officer, of his father's miraculous recovery from cancer. He told us that some years before, his father had been diagnosed with stomach cancer. The exploratory surgery revealed an advanced stage of cancer that had spread to several areas. They had not operated further, but scheduled major surgery for the following month. During those four weeks, Steve's family began a network of prayer. Anyone who did not share the family's belief that prayer could heal was not allowed to visit. He was protected from any negative thinking. Instead, the entire family concentrated on believing that he could and would be healed through prayer, and they affirmed this daily. Thirty days later, when he went in for surgery, the doctor was amazed to find absolutely no evidence of cancer! It was completely gone, and the doctor was unable to explain this astonishing development. Steve assured us that he and his family knew exactly what had cured his father—the power of prayer. He told us not to lose hope, because he had personally experienced the miracle-working power of faith and prayer.

Each of these stories not only provided us with concrete evidence that miracles can and do occur, but they helped validate our belief that we were on the right path, that we were proceeding in the right direction. Each visit, each story seemed to occur at moments when we were particularly depressed, when our spirits were lagging, or when doubt was overtaking us. It was as if the universe were providing us with "manna" to keep us going. Just when we thought we couldn't go any further, someone would appear to share an experience of an actual miracle. I took these as signs that we were on the right path and that the universe was telling us that yes, a miracle was still possible.

A WORD OF HOPE

By 6:00 p.m. Monday evening, Dr. Chaves came to talk with me and Tino about the results of the blood flow test. Much to his surprise, the test revealed an unexpected amount of blood flow still occurring in Deirdre's brain. Based on the steady decline of brain activity as evidence by the EEGs, the medical team had expected there to be very little actual blood flow. He was not sure how to explain it, but there was no doubt as to what the test had revealed. Lack of sufficient blood flow would have signaled that the turning point in the disease had been reached, and recovery was not possible. All other signs indicated that this point had already occurred, and the doctors had expected this test to confirm it. Instead, the test showed that Deirdre's brain was refusing to shut down as it normally does in these cases. It was almost as if she were maintaining some unknown state of "stasis" which could not be explained. Dr. Chaves concluded by saying that we would just have to wait a while longer before we knew anything definite.

Tino and I knew that if the guidance we had received as to why Deirdre had left her body were true, she might need time to gather and evaluate the information she needed. That would explain why the course of her disease was of such long duration and was not progressing according to expected guidelines. Deirdre was stalling, buying time for some reason. That could be the only explanation. We took the results of this test to mean that she still had business to attend to on the spiritual plane and was maintaining her body in a "holding pattern." And this meant that there was still hope. I literally ran down the passageway to the waiting room to share this news with the others.

HEARTS JOINED IN PRAYER

Monday was certainly a busy day for us, what with the many phone calls we engaged in, the information we received, and the steady flow of visitors we welcomed. The people we had actual contact with were not the only source from which we drew hope and strength. We were aware of the many groups in different states that were actively involved in healing efforts. A Catholic church in Chicago held a mass for Deirdre, and candles were lit on her behalf. Throughout the New England/New York area various Wiccan circles performed healing rituals. Different Protestant churches throughout the Midwest were including Deirdre in their weekly prayers, and we, of course, had the prayer support of Silent Unity and the A.R.E. Glad Helpers.

A Unity Meditation. One such group which made a special effort to help was the "Unity Basics" class that Brenda, Sharon, and I had been attending. Mary called us that afternoon to say that the class would render healing prayers for Deirdre that evening. Mary would lead them in a guided meditation for the purpose of sending healing energy. Brenda suggested that we help the process by directing the energy to Deirdre, and it was decided that since Tino and Brenda possessed the best healing abilities, they would stay with Deirdre and try to "channel" this energy directly into her body. Sharon, Dot, Bill, and I would attempt to tune in to this energy flow and direct it to Tino and Brenda. We also called many relatives, explaining that there was going to be a "prayer session" from 7:00 to 7:15 p.m., and asked them to pray along with us at that time.

As 7:00 p.m. drew near, we prepared ourselves for meditation. It is difficult to describe, but I know that I felt a gentle wave of "energy" pass through and around me. I tried to join my thoughts with it and direct it toward Tino and Brenda, sending it through them to Deirdre. A short time later, the feeling subsided and I returned to a state of waking consciousness. Although we used slightly different words to describe this experience, each felt something similar. Tino and Brenda sensed a more intense feeling, such as a pulling of the energy through them and applying it directly to the cells in Deirdre's body.

Mary came to the hospital after class that night, and we discussed our experience. We realized that we were learning to communicate through and work together within the framework of the Universal Mind. A week ago we would not have thought such a thing was possible, but with Deirdre's life at stake, we were following the promptings of Spirit and learning much in the process. We had, in effect, been shown the next step.

This was the first time that we, as a group, had attempted anything of this sort, but it would not be the last. In fact, this step was just the beginning, for we would find ourselves involved in many more such activities before this journey was ended.

GUIDING LIGHTS

The visitors who brightened our days were not the only people who supported us through love and prayer. Our families, although separated by hundreds of miles, were there for us also. Parents, siblings, aunts and uncles, and cousins many times removed were all actively involved in our prayer network and phoned frequently to assure us of their love and support. Tino's sister, Mary; my mother, Esther; my Aunt Ida; and cousin Cheryl were but a few of the many family members who helped us through this difficult time with love and prayer. By trying to remain cheerful and positive when speaking to them, we in effect helped convince ourselves that hope had not died. The religious groups and congregations around the country which were taking time to pray for Deirdre did that much more to strengthen our convictions that a miracle was possible.

The love and support our family, friends, and even total strangers gave to us became our anchor in the storm and helped see us through some of the darkest periods of this ordeal. It was their love, their encouragement, their optimism, and their constant support that sustained us and helped us to stay true to our own faith when doubts assailed us. And it was these wonderful people who were the guiding lights that illuminated our way.

* * *

God has not called us to see through each other, but to see each other through.   —Horace Moody

5

Healers One and All

The only way to discover the limits of the possible is to go beyond them into the impossible. —Arthur C. Clarke

Point of Passage

MONDAY had been a very hectic day. The many phone calls we received and the steady flow of visitors kept us occupied from hour to hour. The results of the blood flow test had given us a positive sign, and we thought this third day had ended on a hopeful note. I even remember thinking that I might get a few good hours of rest that night. This was not to be, however, for there were some odd things going on, things of which we were unaware.

Unknown to anyone, the doctor on duty had spoken to Mary that night and asked her to "prepare the parents," meaning to prepare us for Deirdre's imminent death. Deirdre's brain activity had reached such a low level that the medical team did not believe recovery was possible. Mary was so upset by this development that she could think of nothing to do except stall for time. She asked the doctor to please give us *"just one more day."* When she told us about this weeks later, she said that she hadn't done this out of faith, but out of fear and cowardice. She could not bring herself to tell us this news, nor did she want to be the one to destroy our hopes. Her only option was to stall for time, and so she left without ever giving any indication of what the doctor had said.

I awoke around 2:00 a.m. to find Bill sitting in the waiting room. I thought this strange because he had left for home around 10:00 p.m., and I knew that he planned to go back to work on Tuesday. When I asked him why he had returned, he simply said, "I was told you might need me." Although many of us considered Bill to be the most psychically gifted member of the study group, his response puzzled me because, for all we knew, things seemed to be going well. When I questioned him further, however, he wouldn't say anything more. Although I didn't really understand why he had come back, I was glad he was there.

If I had known the actual reason for Bill's return, it would have no doubt frightened me. Bill had come back because he intuitively knew that Deirdre was rapidly approaching a "passage point" or time of decision. At such times, the soul, through the exercise of free will, is given the opportunity of making a choice to either stay in the earth plane or depart from it. Bill had returned in case Deirdre would make the latter choice that night.

The belief systems of some cultures regard the "mid-morning" hour, halfway between midnight and dawn, as a common time for souls to depart the earth and pass into the spiritual realm. Various religious traditions hold to the belief that death frequently occurs at that time. In the biblical story of the Exodus from Egypt, the Angel of Death was said to have visited sometime between midnight and dawn. Statistics on suicide also seem to support this idea, as a high percentage of suicides occurs around this time.

Brenda, too, was also aware of this impending event, but neither she nor Bill shared this information with anyone. A passage point is only an opportunity for the soul to choose to depart the earth plane. We all face such moments in our lives, sometimes called "death windows." Those souls who have perhaps completed their purpose or those who are too tired to go on use this opportunity to release the physical body and return to their spiritual selves. Others fight mightily to stay, perhaps so that they can complete their life purpose or because of their concern for loved ones who would be left behind. At other times, those who should pass on erroneously try to hang on and linger long after they should have departed the physical world.

Bill and Brenda had no way of knowing what Deirdre would decide. They did not want to unnecessarily alarm anyone or create undue fear, and so they decided not to discuss the matter with those of us who were unaware of what was happening. It was quite possible that Deirdre would let this "passage point" pass without committing to any decision. Fortunately, that is exactly what seems to have happened, for the evening came and went with no discernible change in Deirdre's physical condition.

Brenda's Dream

Perhaps Tino, the others, and I sensed some of what was going on, at least on the subconscious level, because most of us seemed to have difficulty sleeping that night. After talking with Bill awhile, I drifted back to sleep on my cot in the waiting room, only to toss and turn and awake again around 5:00 a.m. The hopeful feeling we'd had the day before had worn off, and for some reason I felt very sad. I couldn't remember what I had been dreaming, but I knew it had left me with an uneasy feeling. I found myself wondering how much longer this waiting game was going to continue. I imagined that Deirdre could remain in a coma for days or perhaps weeks, and I didn't know if I could deal with that. Tino and I were both beginning to wonder how much of Deirdre was still alive and how much of her was being sustained by machines. Neither one of us wanted to prolong her life through artificial means, and we feared that we were rapidly approaching that point.

As we continued to talk, we became aware that Brenda was awake and listening to our conversation. She told us that she had a dream she wanted to discuss. She had asked for guidance before going to sleep and thought that perhaps the dream was meant to help us.

The dream was a simple one. She had dreamt about a baby bottle, an empty baby bottle. She kept looking at the bottle in the dream and thinking that it must hold a clue for us. There was something we needed to learn from it. The symbolism in this dream would have seemed very strange were it not for the visit of a baby to the waiting room the night before. Two of our friends, Tom and Lorna, had brought their newborn son Iain with them when they visited. He was only three weeks old, but Deirdre and I had seen him when we visited Lorna shortly after his birth. Brenda, who has a special fondness for babies, had been particularly enamored of Iain and spent several hours playing with him. Before they left, we had all quietly "blessed the baby" in the manner that Cayce advocated, saying a silent prayer and touching the baby's head. Brenda thought it was possible that Iain had returned the kindness somehow by influencing her dream.

At first, we couldn't make much sense of the dream. We were stumped as to what the significance of an empty baby bottle might be. As we continued to discuss it, however, several possibilities came to light. A baby bottle is the means by which a baby is nourished. It carries the nutrients and food which help a baby to develop and grow. The substance put into the bottle will influence the child's development. It is not the bottle which affects the child's development for that is merely the channel through which the life-giving substances are administered. It is the substance *within* the bottle that brings about growth and change in the child.

Yet the bottle in Brenda's dream was empty. Could it represent an empty channel? Was the dream indicating that we needed to become an empty or open channel? Tino suggested that the bottle was like a hollow tube, a tube through which a substance could flow. If we were the open channels and Deirdre was the child, perhaps the divine power of Spirit was the life-nourishing substance. Perhaps the dream was showing us that we needed to become open channels and allow the life-sustaining, creative energy of Spirit to flow through us to Deirdre. Just as a baby must be fed by means of a bottle, Deirdre must be "nourished" through us acting as open channels for spiritual energy.

FROM THOUGHT TO BELIEF, FROM MIND TO HEART

Now we were even more puzzled, for we thought that this is what we *had* been doing. Upon further examination, however, we came to realize that despite our efforts at prayer and affirmations, we had actually been passive rather than active channels. We had passively prayed and asked God to work the miracle. We had passively affirmed positive conditions and had asked God to bring them about. We had intellectually accepted the power of prayer and faith, and mentally accepted the idea of a miracle as a possibility. We were on the right track, but we hadn't taken this line of thinking far enough. We had come to an *intellectual acceptance* of these beliefs in our minds, but we had not carried it to the next step and *believed from the heart.* This, we realized, was the missing piece of the puzzle.

In order to understand this principle, consider the analogy of building a house. The design of the house first exists as an idea in the mind of a person. The house already exists, but only in the realm of thought. Next, an architect takes this idea and develops a blueprint. The house now exists on paper, but is still not a physical reality. It is only after the builder takes action to pull this idea into reality that it takes form. The house exists in the physical only after the foundation is laid, the lumber for the frame has been cut and fit, and the carpentry completed.

We had conceived the idea of a miracle and perhaps even committed it to a blueprint through our prayers and affirmations, but we had not pulled the idea into reality. We were accepting on the intellectual level of the mind, but not believing from the "beingness" level of the heart. As Sharon so eloquently put it, the distance between mind and heart is small, and on the surface the differences between intellectual acceptance and belief from the heart are subtle. But the energy generated from the heart is one million times more powerful. It is the difference between the idea for a house and the physical completion of that house.

We had given lip service to all the right ideas, but we had not backed up our talk with *right action.* We had been expecting God to do all the work, while we sat back and waited for things to take their course. We had hoped and prayed that God would create a miracle, but we had not taken any steps to become co-creators in this process. We had to move from the level of acknowledging the truth to the level of "being" the truth. It was time to do as Rabbi Pesach Krauss, former chaplain at Memorial Sloan-Kettering Cancer Center, suggests when he advises patients to follow the wisdom of the Jewish sages and "Be a partner with God in creation."[1]

As we reviewed our actions of the last three days, we realized that we were trapped by our own preconceived ideas and expectations as to how things were supposed to be, and this was hampering the free flow of Spirit through us. We hung on to every word the doctors said and had put our faith not in the miracle-working power of Spirit, but in test results! We accepted the doctors' prognosis as to what should happen and believed in their timetables for the course of the disease. We paid an inordinate amount of attention to the monitors surrounding Deirdre because we thought they were an accurate reflection of her condition.

In other words, we were so caught up in the physical illusions of the disease that we could not see the reality of the miracle. While we had accepted the *idea* of a miracle as a possibility, we were giving equal credence and hence power to other possibilities as well! This was why we were experiencing such ups and downs for the past three days. We would correctly start the miracle process, only to sabotage our own efforts by concentrating on the physical illusions of the disease and giving them equal power!

The only way out of this cycle was to implement a course of right action that would enable us to pull the idea of a miracle out of the mental realm of thought and *manifest* it in *reality.* First, it would be necessary to release all our preconceived ideas and expectations of how we thought things should be. Then, following the teachings of *A Course in Miracles*, we would have to deny the physical illusions of our situation and accept a miracle as the only reality. We had to remember that a miracle was not just a possibility, but *the natural order of things.* Next, we had to become open channels and allow Spirit to manifest through us in accordance with divine order and not in the way we expected it should. Finally we had to become an active part of the miracle process and implement a plan of right action. We had to move beyond our *intellectual acceptance* of such things and *believe* from the *"beingness" of our hearts.*

RIGHT ACTION

Right action implies a belief in the divine order of the Universe, which states that the God-Force desires only what is best for each soul. "Best" here means those things, situations, or conditions which will result in the highest good of the soul's spiritual development and will lead the soul to a remembrance of its true oneness with God. By being an open channel and allowing the Spiritual Forces of the universe to flow through you, you allow right action to manifest. You allow the inherent rightness of the God-Force to flow through you so that anything is possible.

As we considered what our plan of right action should be, several elements began to emerge. We realized that we had to:

Implement Right Action.   We had to take an active role and become participants or co-creators in the miracle process.

Be an Open Channel.   First and foremost, we had to remain as empty channels, hollow tubes, through which Spirit would manifest. We could not harbor preconceived ideas as to what we thought should occur or how it should happen. We had to trust Spirit to know what was best and guide us.

See Through Illusion to Reality.   By remaining an open channel, Spirit would enable us to see beyond the illusions of the physical world. This proved to be a very difficult step for most of us. We had to learn to hear what the doctors would say, but not accept it. We had to disregard the findings of their tests because they were only dealing with the physical illusion. And we had to learn to ignore the monitors by Deirdre's bedside, for they, too, only reflected the illusion of the physical world.

This was a very difficult step because we are reared in a world which teaches us the sacredness and inviolability of science. Some might even say our behavior was a form of avoidance or denial. It must be recognized, however, that science operates from a different perception of reality; it operates from the perception of physical law and not spiritual law. So-called "medical miracles" can and do happen every day, as hopeless cases unexpectedly recover and return to full health. The fact that some things defy scientific explanation cannot be denied. Metaphysical sources teach that spiritual law supersedes and transcends the boundaries of physical law and makes these "miracles" possible.

Affirm a Miracle as the Natural Order of Things. We had to stop intellectually accepting the idea of a miracle merely as a possibility and take the next step of believing it to be the natural resolution of the situation.

Create a Visual Focus. We decided that we needed a visual focus or image to symbolize our efforts. The image we chose was a picture of a sunrise, with a rainbow shining above it. Suspended beneath the rainbow was a beautiful red heart. Rays of light shone forth from the sun, illuminating the sky and penetrating the clouds. The rainbow symbolized faith in God's promises, and the heart symbolized love. The sun, of course, symbolized the Universal Spirit, and its rays pierced the clouds of doubt and fear which had obscured our vision. The rainbow was a very important element in this picture because this symbolism had recurred several times during the last three days. Tino bought crayons and drawing paper from the gift shop that morning and sketched this image so that we could hang it in the waiting room.

Act as if the Miracle Had Already Occurred. Finally, we had to act as if we had already received the miracle. One simple demonstration of faith in this regard was to stop the practice of leaving someone in the waiting room at mealtime. By doing this we were actually acknowledging that something "bad" might happen in our absence. From this point on, we ate our meals together, and left Deirdre in God's care.

A TEST OF BELIEF

It wasn't long before the strength of our newly realized convictions would be severely tested. Following the usual morning routine of tests and examination, Dr. Chaves wanted to speak with me and Tino. He had no words of encouragement to give us that morning, for he had come to us with a very different request.

The last EEG showed that the level of activity in Deirdre's brain had decreased significantly. There was no peripheral brain activity, meaning that the cognitive areas of the brain which controlled thinking processes were no longer functioning. The phenobarbital treatment had been unsuccessful, and although they were going to administer it again today, they did not expect it to work. Deirdre had descended to a Level IV Coma, and they felt that there was no chance of recovery. Dr. Chaves didn't explain the details at the time, but we learned later that few people survive a Level III Coma, and those who do normally suffer extensive brain damage. Since Deirdre had lapsed into an even deeper comatose state, past experience told the doctors that there was no hope of recovery.

Dr. Chaves seemed to be fighting back tears as he asked us if we would be willing to sign a "Do Not Revive" (DNR) order. This meant that *if* Deirdre's life signs failed or her heart stopped, the medical team would not make any attempt at revival. They felt that this was in the best interests of everyone, because if she somehow did live, she would exist as little more than a "vegetable" due to the severe damage to her brain function. The medical team felt that it would be more merciful to allow her to die.

We asked Dr. Chaves if he felt we were artificially prolonging Deirdre's life through the machinery of medical technology. Was she "brain dead"? If that was the case, we did not want to sustain her body through artificial means. He answered that no, she was not "brain dead" yet. The blood flow test showed that there was some brain activity although it was at a basal level. This did indicate that she was still fighting, and, as long as that was the case, they would continue to support her. All they were asking for was permission to forgo extensive revival attempts if her bodily functions ceased naturally. Tino and I had already discussed this possibility, and we agreed to sign the papers.

We also told Dr. Chaves that although we heard what he was saying, we knew there was a Higher Power at work and that we would continue to place our belief in that Power. With tears in his eyes and his voice almost cracking, Dr. Chaves thanked us for being "such brave and strong people." He told us that he had never seen this kind of strength and love before. It must have been a strange sight, the parents comforting the doctor, instead of the other way around. But it was Dr. Chaves who appeared to be in need, and so I reached out and gave him a hug, an idea Brenda had suggested earlier. He seemed surprised at first, but he didn't resist. By that time we all had tears in our eyes, but we composed ourselves and signed the papers while Dr. Chaves thanked us for our understanding.

Returning to the waiting room, Tino and I told the others what had just happened. Brenda was the first to react. "Remember, the doctors are working from a *different perception* than we are," she said. "Based on what they believe, Deirdre can't recover. Based on what we believe, she can. Now just take his words and let them flow through you and release them to the universe. Remember, they're only illusion and not reality. Don't give them any power. Shake off that negativity. (Literally.) Now put a big red heart of love over the image of those papers. It doesn't matter that you signed them, because they won't be needed."

Leave it to Brenda to put things into perspective. She had never been one of the so-called "leaders" in study group, but it had become increasingly apparent that she was emerging as the leader during this journey. Time after time she was the person who could pull all the information together, analyze it, and meld it into a cohesive whole. She had become our guide on this journey, and she always seemed to know the right word to help us keep from losing our way and stay true to the path before us.

PRACTICAL APPLICATION

As stated above, an important part of the concept of right action involves becoming participants in the miracle process. This means that it was necessary to put knowledge into action and actually "apply that ye know."[2] But what exactly did we know? We knew that the healing process is essentially an attunement or changing of vibration, and, although healing methods may be applied from "without," the healing or attunement must come from within the self's own mental forces, as the physical, mental, and spiritual levels of being are brought into alignment with the Creative Forces. All healing practices are simply instruments to aid in this process. The task before us was to identify the ways in which we could best help Deirdre achieve this attunement. Not having any formal training, the only thing we knew to do was to employ certain nontraditional or holistic healing methods.

Nontraditional Healing. The practice of using touch, sound, and color to heal the body has existed since ancient times throughout many of the world's cultures. All of these methods are based on the interdependence of body, mind, and spirit and emphasize the use of vibration to change or adjust an imbalance in the body. Western civilization has long ignored these methods as "primitive" teachings. In the last decade, however, so-called "nontraditional" or "alternative" medicine is experiencing a resurgence as modern medicine recognizes the link among mind, emotions, body, and health. Further discoveries in quantum physics on the nature of subatomic particles indicates that all "solid" matter is actually a vibration of energy that gives the appearance of solidity. Alter the vibratory frequency and you alter matter.

Perfect Memory. An important component in a metaphysical understanding of healing is the belief that the microcosm of each cell within the body is a reflection of the macrocosm of the universe. Just as the planets and stars operate according to the laws of force and motion, cells also operate according to set laws. This idea, found in many teachings, was beautifully expressed by the Hopi Indians:

"The living body of man and the living body of the earth were constructed in the same way. Through each ran an axis, man's axis being the backbone, the vertebral column, which controlled the equilibrium of his movements and his functions. Along this axis were several vibratory centers which echoed the primordial sound of life throughout the universe . . . "[3]

Science recognizes this principle as "resonance." All atoms are held together in relationship to all others by a programmed resonant frequency or vibration. This atomic life force or resonant frequency of the body is contained in each cell, programmed according to set patterns or laws established at creation. Disease occurs when the resonant frequency is disrupted, and the cells cannot perform their intended functions. Each cell, however, contains within itself all the information necessary to reactivate this frequency and reconstruct itself when damaged, thus bringing itself into alignment with its intended purpose and function. Each cell, therefore, has "perfect memory" and can in essence heal itself when so directed by the soul force.

Unfortunately, this attribute has long lain dormant, and it must be called to remembrance. We knew the importance of reminding Deirdre that each cell in her body *did* have perfect memory and, when directed by her, could recall the purpose and function for which it was created and restore itself to its proper vibrational frequency.

Up to now we had "talked the talk" about healing, but now it was time to show we could "walk the walk" and put our knowledge and beliefs into action.

WALKING THE WALK

Teamwork. We felt that the first step was to intensify our bedside vigils. After a morning of experimenting with various schedules, we decided that a "team" consisting of at least two people should visit Deirdre every forty minutes. The team was to stay for fifteen to twenty minutes and apply healing methods. In effect, we were carrying our attempt to communicate with Deirdre a step further by adding action to it.

The nursing staff didn't seem to mind this increased level of activity. The ones assigned to attend to Deirdre around-the-clock normally sat no more than a foot from her bed. This morning, however, we noticed that the chair had been pushed back and was several feet from where it had been. We realized that this "distancing" was a necessary defense mechanism against continued emotional attachment to children who would soon die. The nurses believed Deirdre had reached that point, and since they could do nothing more for her, they had no objections to our efforts.

Therapeutic Touch. Knowing that touch, through motion, directly affects vibration, we began a simple regimen of massage as recommended in the Cayce readings. The importance of touch to a person's growth, development, and mental health has long been acknowledged, and the effectiveness of therapeutic touch as an adjunct to healing is gaining increasing recognition. The results of one study have demonstrated that touch increased the production of hemoglobin in the blood and showed that the use of touch helped reduce and alleviate the symptoms of asthma attack. Dr. Lewis Thomas, former director of the Sloan Kettering Cancer Institute, has long advocated that touch is essential to doctoring and urges his fellow physicians to pay more attention to touch and less to probing through instrumentation.

Brenda and Sharon left for a short time and went to a local drug store to buy the ingredients for a therapeutic oil formula[4] given in the Cayce readings. They mixed the ingredients in a baby bottle, and we used the oil to massage Deirdre, paying particular attention to the base of her neck and her liver. We also rubbed it on the soles of her feet, because Mary had indicated that this might be a problem area.

We also used some sand which Jeanne had brought on Sunday. She had gotten this sand during a visit to *El Sanctuario de Nuestro Señor de Esquipulas* in Chimayo, New Mexico. Chimayo is a Roman Catholic shrine where two priests were martyred in the late 1800s and was purported to be the site of a miraculous healing sometime thereafter. It draws thousands of visitors each year and has been called the "Lourdes of America." Over the years, the curative earth from this shrine has been credited with numerous miracles. I had often been skeptical of these types of claims, but by now I was willing to try anything, and we went ahead and put the sand to use.

Music of the Spheres.   We had believed all along that Deirdre would be able to hear us communicate with her, but we had not extended this line of thinking. It suddenly became clear that if she could hear us talk, she could also hear other things going on around her as well. All sound is vibration, and the vibratory energy of sound is well chronicled. Of all sound, music is the most potent vibration and can affect us in ways few other stimuli can. Music can arouse violent passion, "soothe the savage breast," invoke tears or laughter, raise us to the heights of exhilaration, or plummet us to the depths of despair. "It is part of the beauty of the spirit . . . music alone may span that space between the finite and the infinite."[5]

I don't why it took us so long to remember this. Even the

nurses had understood. Deirdre's corner area of the pediatric ICU was equipped with an overhead television, and the nurses often turned it on, particularly late at night when there was little other activity. They said patients enjoyed hearing the sound, even though they might not appear to be aware of it. We realized that we, too, could use the healing vibration of music by playing audiotapes for Deirdre.

As we were setting up a cassette player, one of the residents, East Indian in origin, asked us what we were doing. When we explained that we thought Deirdre would be able to hear the music, he smiled and told us that that was quite possible. *He* suggested that we bring in some of *her* favorite tapes, because she would be more likely to respond to music she enjoyed. This doctor was evidently familiar with certain aspects of nontraditional medicine.

Color Therapy. The importance of color and its influence upon humans is well established. It has been repeatedly demonstrated that certain colors can evoke specific emotions and responses. People express a great deal of concern over the color schemes in their homes, hospitals use color to achieve certain effects, and even restaurants such as McDonald's have based their color schemes upon color studies. Yet despite the body of knowledge concerning the effects of color upon humans, the vibratory aspect of color is often overlooked even though *"color is but vibration."*[6]

Understanding that the vibratory frequency of a color ray can penetrate both the aura and the body at the cellular level, we thought it would be helpful to apply a form of color therapy by coordinating the color of the clothing we wore. First, we determined the atmosphere most needed that day and then matched it with the color which would evoke that circumstance. The emphasis right now was on healing, so we chose the color green. As circumstances changed, we would wear other colors to evoke different moods, such as red for energy and pink for love.

A Matter of Perception. As we applied these various

healing practices, we continued to talk to Deirdre as we had done before. Now, however, we added a new dimension to our conversation. We not only explained to Deirdre what we were doing, but we told her not to listen to any negative comments the doctors or nurses might say in her presence. We realized that they often discussed Deirdre's condition amongst themselves, and it occurred to us that if she could hear us, she could hear them as well. It was even possible that all of our positive comments were being nullified every time the medical team discussed further deterioration in her condition. We explained that the medical staff was working from a different physical perception, whereas we were working from the reality of spirit.

Novice Healers

We had begun these efforts somewhat tentatively. This was not something any of us had tried before, and we learned through a process of trial and error. It may sound strange, but several of us began to have the feeling that we had done something similar a very long time ago, and this feeling would grow in intensity as the days progressed. It was almost as if long-forgotten memories were beginning to surface to help direct our actions.

The universal forces of Spirit were also working with us, for Tuesday marked the day several "true healers" arrived at the hospital and offered their help. Once again, some were friends, while others were strangers who had heard about Deirdre and had come to help. Their arrival was most timely and welcomed, for it coincided with our own meager efforts at healing, and we took this as confirmation that we were progressing on the right path.

Medicine Woman

The first "healer" to visit Tuesday was Jan Snyder, the

woman who had received information about Deirdre during a drumming trance. She arrived in the late morning and asked if she could apply some prayer/healing practices in the Native American tradition. She spent quite some time with Deirdre and felt that the visit confirmed the information she had received during the trance. Like Mary, she paid special attention to the areas of the brain stem and the liver. Before she left, she placed a Native American amulet in Deirdre's hand. It was a stone sewn into a leather "pouch" suspended at the end of a leather strap, designed to be worn about the neck. The pouch was decorated with beadwork and fringing. Jan asked that we keep the amulet in Deirdre's hand. The river rock stone, she said, had great healing powers.

We thanked Jan for her visit and she told us that she would continue to pray for Deirdre. Later, one of the nurses saw the amulet and asked its purpose. When we told her it was supposed to have healing powers, she thought for a moment and then responded, *"Oh, that's right, her father is Indian, isn't he?"* This fact had also helped explain the large amethyst crystal which Tino had placed next to her bedside. We were beginning to realize that if hospital personnel thought something was of Native American origin, they were much more likely to accept it without further question.

HANDS-ON HEALING

Shortly after Jan left, we were visited by the first of two separate groups who came to offer their help with what is often commonly called "hands-on healing." Each group belonged to a different church, although the churches were both within the Pentecostal tradition. These denominations profess a strong belief in the power of the Holy Ghost to bring about healing. They claim to be able to channel this power and through touch send it directly into a person's body.

I had never considered the possibility that this is actually a form of metaphysical healing, and I must admit that I didn't have a very favorable opinion of these religious groups. My own opinion was clouded by my bias toward what I considered restrictive beliefs and a sometimes self-righteous attitude. Although I had never outwardly showed it, I sometimes felt that the nickname "holy-rollers" fit them quite well because of what I considered overzealous behavior. Yet now, people with whom I once thought I had nothing in common had come to join with us in Spirit. The irony of this did not escape me, as I realized that this was yet another learning situation.

The First Wave. The first group was led by James, a navy hospital corpsman who was also a certified emergency medical technician. We had talked about religion a few times, and I knew that he had deep religious beliefs. He knew that I was a Christian, although I had never discussed any of my metaphysical beliefs with him. James was accompanied by Nancy, a civilian with whom we worked, and Kim, another navy member. As we talked about God, the Holy Ghost, prayer, and miracles, I realized that their beliefs were really not that different from mine. We might use different words to describe the same phenomena, but we all believed in the reality of Spirit and its power over the physical.

James had come in the hope of being allowed to perform an actual hands-on healing. Despite our talks on religion he was not sure how I would receive this idea, but felt compelled to make the attempt. He seemed relieved that we did share a similar belief that prayer could help heal Deirdre.

As we had other visitors, Brenda took this group into the pediatric ICU. It took a total of forty minutes to complete the session, and Brenda described it to us afterward. First, James quickly read Deirdre's medical chart and monitors. He instructed the others to place their hands on Deirdre, and he proceeded to walk around them. He seemed to be talking to himself as he did this. Brenda thought he might even be "speaking in tongues" although his words were inaudible. He paid attention to both the brain stem and the liver. By now there was no doubt that each healer intuitively knew which areas of Deirdre's body had been most affected by the disease.

Brenda told us that she could feel a great deal of energy as James worked, and the temperature grew increasingly hot. Kim was fairly new to this and couldn't understand why the room had suddenly become so warm. Even a nurse commented about the unusual heat. We knew that the heat was a result of the energy patterns James had generated. Brenda commented that he possessed a great deal of healing ability and had certainly demonstrated an advanced knowledge of working with Spirit.

Reinforcements. While this was taking place, a second group of healers arrived. This group was led by Simon, another navy member. He was accompanied by Robin, a member of his church. They had come for the same reason as the previous group, and we talked about much the same things. I told Simon that I would welcome his help, and he could see Deirdre as soon as the first group was finished.

When Brenda emerged from the pediatric ICU, the last thing she expected to see was another group of healers waiting to go in! *"More?"* she asked, her surprise showing. *"There's more?"* Simon and Robin were joined by Nancy, who had decided to participate in the second session. Simon used a different, more verbal approach than James had. He had everyone hold hands while he prayed over Deirdre. He sensed the energy that James had raised and commented upon the strong presence of the Holy Spirit that he felt.

While Simon prayed over Deirdre, James and I spoke for a while longer, and he told me that "The Holy Spirit is strong in there," meaning the pediatric ICU. "I felt its presence throughout the room. And," he said, "I sense many angels are here to help. We're not alone." Then he told me that his church was going to hold a special service for Deirdre that evening. They were calling in "twelve of our best healers," and they, along with the congregation, would direct the healing energy of the Holy Spirit to Deirdre. I told him what we had done the night before during the "Unity Basics" prayer service, and he agreed that it might be helpful to try that approach again. After joining in a short prayer, he and Kim departed.

Simon's group stayed with Deirdre for more than a half-hour. When they returned to the waiting room, Simon asked if we would hold hands and join in prayer. We had several other visitors at the time, and they joined us as well. As he proceeded to pray in a rather loud voice, I was aware that we received some curious looks from passersby and others in the waiting room. This was not the first time, and I knew it would probably not be the last, that we drew curious stares and wondering glances.

Tears of a Friend

Late afternoon marked the visit, not of a healer, but of a friend who was in need of healing herself. Eleven-year-old Jenny was our next-door neighbor and Deirdre's best friend. They spent a lot of time together, and Jenny was often at our house, which she seemed to think of as her own. I often caught her rummaging through the refrigerator and cabinets in search of food as if she owned the place. She called our house "the place to eat," and she spent so much time with Deirdre that I sometimes called her my "other daughter."

Unfortunately, over a month prior to Deirdre's illness, she and Jenny had a major "falling out." It was not like their usual tiffs and spats which barely lasted more than a day; this seemed to be a serious break in their friendship. It involved not only Jenny, but several other of Deirdre's friends as well. Deirdre had broken off relationships with all of her friends and had, in effect, isolated herself from all social contact for the last several weeks. At first I thought it was a result of normal disagreements that girls that age often have, but as it continued I became concerned. Deirdre, however, assured me that she didn't need or want my interference, and I thought it best to let her resolve the situation herself.

It wasn't until weeks later, when reading an article on Reye's syndrome, that I came across information about this "distancing behavior." Evidently, some children who contract Reye's show this type of isolationist behavior a few days before the onset of the disease. What was so unusual in Deirdre's case was that this behavior had begun about five weeks prior to the onset of Reye's. As I look back on it now, it almost seemed as if she had been purposely distancing herself from close friends, perhaps in anticipation of the coming crisis.

Whatever the reason, it was obvious that Jenny was now feeling a tremendous amount of guilt over what had happened, almost to the point of blaming herself for Deirdre's illness. Jenny's mother Carol told me that Jenny's greatest fear was that Deirdre would die before she could tell her how sorry she was.

I talked to Jenny and told her that there was no reason to blame herself for anything. The fact that Deirdre had gotten sick had nothing to do with their fight. I tried to reassure her that Deirdre did know how much she loved her and assured her that Deirdre loved her like a sister as well. I told her that even family members sometimes have misunderstandings, but that doesn't change their love for one another. As we talked, her tears lessened, and I believe she felt a little bit better.

Carol thought it best that Jenny not see Deirdre, connected to tubes and machines as she was, and I agreed. I told Jenny that even though Deirdre was in a coma, we thought that she could hear us, and I would tell her that she had come to visit and let her know what we talked about. I took the cards she had brought from Deirdre's class, one from each student, and told her I would take these in with me so that I could let Deirdre know what the class had done.

Carol asked me to keep in close touch and let her know if there were any changes. Jenny asked if there was anything else she could do, and I told her that it would help if she would pray. She said she already was. As they left, my heart went out to this little girl carrying such a heavy load of guilt and pain.

ANOINTING OILS

Another unexpected visitor that day was Reverend Winn, an associate pastor of a local First Assembly of God Church. A total stranger, he presented his card and told me that he was the pastor of the church attended by the brother of an officer I worked with—the same Steve who shared the story of his father's cancer cure with us. I knew Steve, of course, but I didn't know his brother or have any connection with his brother's church. This was just another example of how news of our plight had spread by word of mouth. And although I didn't understand the connection, he was accompanied by James's wife Karen, who had been unable to come earlier with her husband.

Reverend Winn told us his congregation had been praying for Deirdre, and that he had come to ask if he might be permitted to "anoint Deirdre with oils." He explained that this was a common practice within his religion and was based on the biblical tradition of using anointing oil from the time of Abraham to the time of Christ. He shared several biblical passages with us:

"The Spirit of the Lord God is upon me, because the Lord has anointed me to bring good tidings to the afflicted." (Isaiah 61:1)

". . . and shows steadfast love to his anointed." (Psalm 18:50)

". . . Thou anointest my head with oil, my cup runneth over." (Psalm 23:5)

"How God anointed Jesus of Nazareth with the Holy Spirit and with power; how he went about doing good and healing all that were oppressed." (Acts 10:38)

When I told Reverend Winn that I would be happy to have him anoint Deirdre, he seemed relieved. I think that he expected he would have to convince us of the validity of his request and was surprised that we seemed to understand and accept his offer so quickly. We talked about the power of the Holy Spirit and its ability to bring about miracles. Then he allowed Karen to accompany him, but asked that they be left alone. At first I was a little hesitant to allow this, but I knew that Deirdre always had a nurse nearby, and so I agreed. After about fifteen minutes, they returned to the waiting room. Before they left, Reverend Winn assured me that he and his congregation would continue to keep Deirdre in their prayers.

A Moment's Pause

By dinner time, we ourselves were left pondering the strange sequence of events unfolding around us. The oddity of the day's events became clear when we tried to explain them to Tino and Darcie. Tino had been gone most of the day and missed several of our visitors. He had left after Jan's visit to go check on Darcie, run some errands, and pick up clean clothing and tapes for Deirdre. He had returned with Darcie shortly before the healing service was scheduled to begin. Darcie was feeling better and had insisted upon coming to the hospital if only for a few hours. We hurriedly tried to explain what had happened, but the looks on their faces told us how incredulous it must have sounded.

By now, however, the unusual was becoming commonplace, and we knew that many of our visitors that day had raised eyebrows and were the focus of quiet speculation. A medicine woman, a pastor with anointing oils, hands-on healers, and people in navy uniforms had made for a strange array of characters. Add to this the constant stream of visitors, the frequent and sometimes strange phone calls we received, our "rainbow" picture on display, and the curious nature of our conversations, it did make for an interesting spectacle. Several nurses would later tell us that they had never experienced anything like it in all their years of nursing.

Yet the sudden appearance of so many different "healers" helped to convince us that our plan of right action was correct, and we were working in attunement with Spirit. We awaited the church service with eager anticipation.

The Power of the Holy Spirit

As we had done prior to the Unity prayer service, we called many relatives and friends and asked them to pray at the same time the healing service was scheduled. Then shortly before its start, Tino, Brenda, Sharon, Dot, Bill, and Darcie joined me in preparation for meditation. Unfortunately, the consultation room was locked and Sharon, Darcie, and I ended up in a stairwell so that we could have some privacy. Once again Tino and Brenda were at Deirdre's bedside. I think we all expected a similar experience, but this time we would each feel a much different sensation from what we had the night before.

At first, I wasn't able to feel anything and was having difficulty concentrating. Suddenly, like a train approaching at full throttle, I sensed an enormous "wave" of energy flow around me. It moved so quickly that I couldn't tap into it. It was as though it was so powerful it didn't need any assist from me. Those of us who were meditating described a similar sensation.

While our meditations ended within fifteen minutes, it was more than forty-five minutes before Tino and Brenda emerged from the pediatric ICU, and it was obvious from their appearance that something had happened. They were flushed and their hands trembled as they described feeling a strong wave of energy sweep through them. It was all they could do to keep their attention focused on sending the energy through to Deirdre. The experience had left them drained and exhausted, and a tingling sensation was still present in their hands. They had apparently absorbed a great deal of energy and were still retaining some of it, which they felt needed to be released. They took hold of my and Sharon's hands and sent the excess energy through to us. We did feel energized by this and went in to see Deirdre so that we could continue to channel this energy to her.

It was obvious that the energy generated by this healing service was very different from that generated by the Unity prayer service the night before. This was an intense, emotional type of energy, which swept right through us, and it certainly didn't need our direction or focus. There was no doubt in our minds that these people certainly knew how to access the power of the Holy Spirit and channel its energy. I gained a new respect for this religious tradition that evening and realized that, in some ways, they were far beyond us in their understanding and application of the workings of Spirit.

MANY PATHS, ONE DESTINATION

Our journey this day led us into an area where trails converged and crossed as they carved out their individual routes of spiritual unfoldment. Our path was but one of many, each distinct in its own right, but each proceeding to the same destination at the mountain's summit. Each path gave the traveler a different view or perspective, but regardless of how they got there, all travelers would reach the same point at the end of their travels.

Perhaps the lesson here was that we are not alone; other

pilgrims are making similar journeys although they may be following different routes. When diverse paths cross, we can either delay one another by emphasizing our differences or we can expand our vision and recognize our oneness in Spirit. By doing this, we take a step forward in consciousness and thus expedite our journey up the mountain. Perhaps the key to continued advancement is to learn that despite our differences, our purpose is the same. We are all seeking the road back to our true spiritual home. We must learn to cast aside fear and distrust and live life in the spirit of understanding and love.

✳ ✳ ✳

There are a variety of gifts, but the same Spirit.
There are varieties of service, but the same Lord . . .
In each of us the Spirit is manifested in one particular way,
*   for some useful purpose . . .*
But all gifts are the work of one and the same Spirit.
                                        —I Corinthians 12:4, 5, 7, 11

6

Love in Action

And now abide Faith, Hope, Love, these three. But the greatest of these is Love. —I Corinthians 13:13, NKJV

TUESDAY'S events taught us a very important lesson and provided us with an ideal example of the power of love. The many people who appeared to help us were motivated by a sincere desire to be of service to others. Their words of comfort, hope, and faith, and their willingness to support us in every way possible provided a perfect demonstration of the universal law of love.

THE UNIVERSAL LAW OF LOVE

Love is perhaps the most widely discussed yet most misunderstood of all emotions. While the English language has only one word to express the concept of love, other languages are more precise and use specific words to denote different types of love. The ancient Greeks, for example, differentiated among three kinds of love: *eros* meaning romantic love, *philia* expressing the concept of brotherly love, and *agape* to denote the love of God. When we speak of the universal law of love, we are referring to *agape*. Love in this sense refers to universal or divine love, sometimes called unconditional love.

Love in this sense is selfless and nonjudgmental. It accepts people as they are, not because of who they are or in spite in what they are. It is given freely and asks nothing in return. It is the love expressed by the Creator and the gift or birthright given to all souls at the time of creation. Unconditional love allows us to see others as our Creator sees them, a perfect expression of God. By learning to put aside the limiting, selfish motives of ego and allowing the higher or soul-self to manifest, we can experience the transforming quality of love.

The Cayce readings state that the basis of all universal law can be summed up in three words: GOD IS LOVE. This does not mean that God loves or that God can love or that God chooses to love or that God might love you if you behave in a certain way. All of these ideas limit love and imply that God can withhold love. Yet these spiritual teachings say that God IS love. Love defines God; it is the every essence of what God IS. And since love is God, it is the source from which all creation flows and the force through which the universe itself was brought into being. It was through love that God extended a portion of Himself to bring companion souls into creation. We are each an individualized expression of that perfect love, life, and intelligence.

The Dynamic Quality of Love.   The universal law of love can be expressed as "that dynamic force which brings into manifestation all things. It is the healing force, the cleansing force, and the force that blesses all things we touch."[1] "The first law of love is: Love transforms."[2] But how can love be a dynamic or creative force that brings about change? The answer to this may be found in the idea that " . . . perfect love casteth out fear." (I John 4:18)

Fear is the emotion from which all negative conditions, such as hate, anger, and resentment, arise. By replacing fear with love, we allow the free flow of the Spirit of love to manifest through us. We understand that everything is working together for good and that each condition is a lesson that must be learned. When we face the conditions of life with love, we align ourselves with the Creative Forces which can effect change in our lives. When love is brought into a circumstance, the condition, situation, or relationship will be changed. It will be uplifted and transformed. The renowned theologian, Teilhard de Chardin, expressed this dynamic quality thus: "Someday, after we have mastered the winds, the waves, the tide, and gravity, we shall harness for God the energies of love. Then, for the second time in the history of the world, man will have discovered fire."[3]

Love, Healing, and Miracles.   The transforming power of love is the birthright given to each soul at the moment of creation and is thus available to everyone. Its power is unlimited. The link between love and emotional healing has long been noted by practitioners in the mental health field. Dr. Frances Vaughn, former president of the Association for Transpersonal Psychology, states: "We are teaching and learning more about the power of love in healing. . . When we bring love into awareness, we invite healing."[4]

In recent years, medical professionals have begun to acknowledge the link between love and physical healing as well. The transforming quality of love has been repeatedly addressed by the well-known author and physician Dr.

Bernie S. Siegel. In his book *Love, Medicine, and Miracles*, he states that "Unconditional love is the most powerful stimulant of the immune system. The truth is: love heals . . . Miracles happen to exceptional patients every day . . . When one believes in love and miracles, divine intervention can occur . . . one generation's miracle may be another's scientific fact."[5]

Dr. Larry Dossey, in his book *Healing Words*, writes of the growing body of evidence indicating that love is crucial in the healing process: "Love is intimately related with health. Love moves the flesh . . . The power of love to change bodies is legendary."[6]

Unconditional love, then, appears to be a key to the healing process and hence the creation of miracles. Unconditional loves begins by our learning to forgive both ourselves and others, learning to see the Universal Spirit in all we meet, and learning to give from the heart without expectation of anything in return. Unconditional love enables us to become part of the creative process not by exerting our own will with its limited vision, but by releasing people and situations to the all-knowing wisdom of the Universal Spirit.

Release to Love

Release is perhaps the most difficult step of the healing process. Contrary to what many people believe, release does not mean a "giving up" or a defeatist attitude of resignation. Rather, release is action. It is the opening of the door that, up to this point, has blocked the entry of a Higher Power into our lives. The third step of Alcoholics Anonymous's 12-Step Program expresses the active element of release:

"We MADE A DECISION to turn our will and our lives over to the care of a Higher Power, as we understood it."[7]

The decision to open this door does not come easily, because the locks and chains which bind it are woven from the fabric of what we erroneously believe to be our true selves—the ego or lower self—and people do not want to give up what they believe to be their identity. We need to realize, however, that by opening this door, we will allow our true selves—the Higher Self—to be expressed, and by bringing the ego under its control, we gain true independence of spirit as we allow divine activity to become a part of our lives.

The key to opening this door requires a willingness to let divine activity express itself through us. When we stop trying to *control life* and realize that we *belong to life*, we become a part of life's creative process. We do not lose control, but actually gain it on a higher plane as we align our will with Divine Will. By releasing the ego, we reclaim our birthright as spiritual beings and thus regain control of our destiny as co-creators and companions to God. "I and the Father are One." (John 10:30)

Tino and I had been truly blessed to be surrounded by so many people who were able to let go of the limited vision of their own egos and allow Divine Spirit to direct their actions. Each person who came to help was motivated not by any selfish reason or hope of personal gain, but by the selfless motivation of unconditional love. There was nothing to be gained from their actions other than to help a fellow human being in need. They saw a child in need of healing and were able to set aside their differences and unite in the spirit of love to meet that need. They reached out in love and compassion, and extended a part of themselves in an attempt to help another. They knew that it was only through the healing power of the spirit of love that a miracle would be possible.

Following their example, we knew it was time for us to respond to Deirdre in kind. We had prayed for and received guidance. We had initiated a plan of right action and opened ourselves to the flow of Spirit through us so that we could become a part of the miracle process. We had done everything we could, and now it was time to take the final step. We had to have the courage to put aside our own needs, wants, and expectations, and love Deirdre enough to release her to her highest good. We had to let go and let God express Himself through Deirdre in perfect ways.

RELEASE TO A HIGHER POWER

The idea of releasing Deirdre to her highest good had come up Tuesday morning when we were discussing the need for right action. We had actually discussed it several days earlier, but I think it was something that most of us just gave lip service to. We did not mean it from the heart. At least, that was true for me. I wanted one thing and one thing only, and that was to have my daughter recover and return to me. I didn't want to consider any other possibility. And even though I knew that my own insight was limited and that I couldn't possibly understand all the variables at work, it didn't matter. I just wasn't ready to accept the idea that recovery might not be in Deirdre's best interests.

I knew the importance of "letting go and letting God," but I couldn't bring myself to take that final step. I was still holding on. I had even tried to cajole God into seeing it my way by reminding Him that people needed proof of miracles, and He had the perfect opportunity to demonstrate one here! I may have ended my prayers with "Thy will be done," but I wasn't feeling it in my heart.

Then late Tuesday night, after all our visitors had left and the commotion of the day had settled down, Brenda suggested that Tino and I, along with Darcie, leave and go home for the night. As soon as she said it, Sharon, Dot, and Bill enthusiastically embraced the idea. It would be a perfect demonstration of faith, they said, of belief that the miracle had already happened. It would demonstrate that we had truly released Deirdre into God's care. They would stay the night at the hospital, and we would go home. When I heard this suggestion, I was horrified! Leave my daughter and go home? No way! I couldn't, I wouldn't desert her! She needed me. How could they even suggest such a thing?

Then much to my surprise, both Tino and Darcie agreed with the idea. I couldn't believe it! Didn't they understand what they were asking me to do? I was determined to fight them on this and I did, for several hours. But then, from somewhere deep within me, I heard the still, small voice which told me that I needed to let go. I didn't want to listen to my little voice either, and I began to argue with it. I can't leave, I told it. What if I leave and something happens . . .

What if something happens. There it was. My fear of "losing" my daughter. My fears were still with me. I hadn't been able to set them aside. I didn't want to leave because I was afraid that something might happen. I was still trying to hold on and control the situation. I didn't have enough faith to take the final step and let go. Yet I knew that I must.

And so, with a heavy heart, I went to Deirdre and told her that I would be going home for a few hours that night. I told her that I knew she was in God's hands and that was the best possible place for her. I told her I would be with her in Spirit and that I would come to see her as soon as I got back the next morning. Then I left, hoping that by performing the action, I would manifest the belief. It was not as easy as that, however, and I soon found myself confronting my own Dark Night of the Soul.

THE DARK NIGHT OF THE SOUL

The Dark Night of the Soul[8] must come into the experience of each individual. It is the time of meeting self, the time of harvesting the seeds we have sown. It is the hour of doubt, the hour of fear, the moment when you can endure no more. Even the Master confronted this dark night as He prayed to the Father to *"take this cup away from me"* in the Garden of Gethsemane. (Matthew 26:39)

As a metaphor, Dark Night refers to a time when we face away from the light. We are surrounded by fears and temptations and cannot see a way out. Hope appears to be gone and faith waivers. It is the hour during which the patient, whose body wracked by cancer, can no longer bear the pain and cries, *"No more!"* It is the hour that the soldier, forced to take an enemy's life, cries out, *"Forgive me!"* It is the hour a young child learns of the death of his father and cries out, *"Why?"* It is the hour the alcoholic, dying a slow death, looks upward and pleads, *"Help me!"* And it is the hour a parent, faced with the death of a child, cries without words, for even words have lost their meaning.

We all encounter our own Dark Night of the Soul. We can either succumb to the fears and doubts which surround us, or we can recognize this Dark Night for the stepping-stone it is and pass through the trials of the night and into the truth and light of day. The only way to safely pass through this hour is to release it to a Higher Power and say, "Thy will, not mine, be done."

Thy Will Be Done.   My own Dark Night of the Soul began as we left the hospital that evening. As we drove home, I couldn't escape the sick feeling in the pit of my stomach. I was resentful at being "forced" away, and I was angry at myself for going. All my fears and doubts were surfacing, and I couldn't ignore them any longer.

When I arrived home, with Tino and Darcie, for the first time in four days, the many reminders of Deirdre's presence only intensified my feelings of guilt and hopelessness. Tino wanted to do a load of laundry—his way of dealing with the situation was to keep busy. There was no way I could fall asleep, and so Darcie and I sat down to talk. I saw Deirdre's favorite doll "Huggie," a Hugga-Bunch® doll, lying on the floor. I started to cry as I remembered how she had wanted that particular doll because it was one of the few that looked like her, with dark hair and eyes. I held the doll tightly as we talked, wondering if Deirdre would ever return home to play with her again.

We talked about memories of happier times, but mostly we talked about our fears. I remember admitting my fear that Deirdre was going to die and saying that I didn't know how I could handle that loss. I told Darcie I didn't want to leave the hospital because I was afraid she was going to die while I was gone, and I would never forgive myself for not being there. We tried to reassure each another, through our tears, that everything was going to be all right. I think that by trying to convince one another, we ended up reassuring ourselves.

As we continued to talk about the difference between releasing Deirdre to her highest good and just plain giving up, I realized that Darcie was having similar feelings. The more we spoke, the more I tried to convince both of us that it was the right thing to do. We finally came to the point of asking what was best for Deirdre, and it was then that I finally faced the root of my greatest fear. What if it would be best for Deirdre if she not recover? What if it would be better for her to pass on?

This, then, was my darkest hour. What was best for me, meaning Deirdre's recovery and return, might not be what was best for her. Was my love for her great enough to put her needs above mine, even if it meant accepting the alternative which would bring me the greatest sorrow? Did I love her enough to honor her soul's choice and let her go?

As I asked myself these questions, my will, the ego will, finally began to break down, and I realized with horror that by holding on I had been putting my needs above those of my daughter. I was acting out of selfishness and putting "me" first. This realization shook me to the very foundations of my reality and "brought me to my knees." I felt ashamed and worthless, broken and humbled. Was this the quality of my love?

Yet in my heart of hearts I really did want what was best for Deirdre, and if that meant accepting a choice other than my own, so be it. In that one brief moment, I realized that it was because of my love for her that I must let her go. So, I released her in love and knew, in my heart, that I had truly done it.

It is hard to explain what I felt after that. After I voiced my greatest fears, it was as if they ceased to have any power over me. I was no longer anxious and distressed. It was as if a sense of calm acceptance had taken hold, and I intuitively knew that all things were working together for good. What I had feared as surrender was, in fact, a step toward taking control. As the Tao teaches, "You must yield to overcome."

I said a prayer before falling asleep, and in it I told Deirdre that I loved her enough to honor her decision, whatever it would be. I knew that, wherever she was, she was in Spirit and had at her disposal all the information necessary to make the decision which would be for the highest good of all concerned.

The remaining hours of the night passed without incident. We awoke around 6:00 a.m., gathered up new clothing and returned to the hospital. Brenda and Sharon were just waking up as we got there. Tino and I immediately went in to see Deirdre, and I asked the nurse on duty how she had been during the night. I knew that the pressure in Deirdre's brain had reached the extremely high level of thirty-six on Tuesday, while her blood pressure and pulse dropped to dangerously low levels and her temperature fluctuated between fever and subnormal readings. I had expected this to continue throughout the night. Even though none of the doctors had said anything specific, I knew that many expected that she would not survive the night.

Much to my surprise, however, the night had been quiet. "Actually," the nurse said, "it's been an uneventful night. Her vital signs were stable, and her pulse was steady."

It seemed that, despite my fears and heightened emotions, Deirdre had spent a peaceful night, with little change in her condition. I don't know if it was with relief or dread that I realized the waiting game was going to continue a while longer.

SHOW ME A SIGN

The physical and emotional strain of the last four days had taken a toll on everyone. In addition to the sheer exhaustion we all felt, many of us were beginning to come down with coughs, colds, and other illness symptoms. I know that more than one of us was beginning to wonder how much longer we could endure this situation of constant waiting. If only we had a concrete sign to help us keep going.

Wednesday morning, Brenda surveyed the situation and realized that we couldn't go on this way much longer. In an act of quiet desperation she went in alone to Deirdre and, speaking out loud, told her we needed a sign to show us that she wanted to return. The sign had to be distinct and clearly indicate to Brenda that it was not just her imagination. Without a sign, Brenda would assume that Deirdre did not want to return, and we would honor that decision.

We only found out later what happened. As Brenda's mouth fell open in amazement, Deirdre gave not one, but three distinct signs. First, there was visible eye movement beneath her eyelids and she tried to open her eyes. Second, she turned her head toward Brenda and moved it straight up. Finally, she lifted her right arm in the air and then put it down. At first Brenda thought she was imagining all this, but the three signs convinced her that they were real. Then she told Deirdre that she would have to help us so that we would know what to do next. "I don't remember how to help you come back," Brenda said.

Within moments, Darcie entered the pediatric ICU. Brenda believed that Darcie had been "sent" by Deirdre to help in some way. When Darcie heard what had just happened, she wanted to run to the cafeteria, where Tino and I were having breakfast, and tell us what had happened. Brenda stopped her, believing that this was not a good idea. Brenda had seen us go through too many ups and downs the last four days, and she wasn't willing to put us through that again. She wanted to wait until there was something more concrete. But she did know that it was time to take some action and help bring Deirdre home.

Darcie's response was to go into the rest room located directly next to the pediatric ICU. One wall of the restroom actually bordered the corner of the ICU where Deirdre lay, forming the wall directly behind her bed. There, from a distance of less than three feet, Darcie proceeded to perform a ritual, in the Wiccan tradition, for the purpose of directing energy. Knowing that Deirdre had given hopeful signs, she concentrated on sending her strength and energy to help her fight her way back.

Shortly after Darcie left to perform the ritual, Brenda's husband Brad arrived. It was the first time he had come to see Deirdre. He had been busy working sixteen hours a day and taking care of their eleven-year-old daughter Sara. Brad didn't realize how ill Deirdre was and he had become quite angry with Brenda for staying with us at the hospital. When he saw Deirdre, comatose and hooked up to tubes and machines, he was shocked and felt guilty about his resentments. He started to cry. Brenda didn't want to expose Deirdre to this negativity, and so she sent him out of the ICU. I remember him returning to the waiting room looking like a sad little boy.

Brenda stayed with Deirdre then, still wondering how to help her come back. Deirdre seemed so weak and tired. It was as if she wanted to return, but didn't have the strength to do so. She needed some energy.

Energy! The realization washed over Brenda like a tidal wave battering a ship. Deirdre needed energy! It was no coincidence that Brad had arrived shortly after Deirdre's three signs. Brad was the source of energy she needed!

ENERGY TRANSFER

We all knew that Brad possessed an inordinate amount of energy. He consistently worked seventy to eighty hours per week and was seldom able to sit still for more than a few moments. Brad also held a lot of anger within him, and at times this anger would explode in intense bursts of energy felt by all those in his path. We had often felt that if that energy could be channeled in a positive way, its effects could be tremendous. Now was the time to harness that energy and apply it in a positive way.

Brenda literally ran out of the pediatric ICU and into the waiting room, grabbed Brad by the arm, and pulled him back into the ICU. "Come on, Brad," she said. "I need you in here."

Once at Deirdre's bedside, Brenda instructed Brad to touch Deirdre, hold her hand, and send all the energy he could into her body. Brad asked Brenda to give him specifics, and she suggested he do what Mary had done—put one hand behind the base of her neck and the other over the stomach area. He spent the next thirty minutes concentrating on sending all his excess energy to Deirdre. Brad had never been very interested in anything metaphysical and had never even come close to doing anything like this before. I don't know what amazed him more, the fact that Brenda had asked him to help or the fact that he was doing it.

When they returned to the waiting room, Brenda told us what they had done. She still didn't mention the three signs she had seen, but it made sense to us that Brad could help Deirdre by sending energy. In fact, he was still so energized that Brenda suggested he send some of his excess energy to me. As he sat beside me and placed his hands on my shoulders, I could feel the warmth of the energy flowing through my body as it brought strength and vitality. Brad certainly possessed a gift of great potential.

A PUPIL RESPONSE

The doctor's routine visit that morning was conducted by Dr. Lillian Pardo, who had taken over as presiding doctor while Dr. Chaves was off for the next two days. Dr. Pardo's demeanor was very different than that of Dr. Chaves's; her manner was much more upbeat and lively. She told us that Deirdre was stable, with no major change in her condition, and that her pulse was steady. She would keep close watch on the case and let us know if there were any changes.

Shortly after lunch, Dr. Pardo called Tino and I into the pediatric ICU. It seemed that there had been a development. As Tino and I braced for the worst, she told us that they had detected a pupil response in the left eye. A review of Deirdre's chart showed Dr. Pardo that this was the first time such a response had been detected since admission. It could be "a good sign," she told us, but she wanted to wait longer to see if the other eye would begin to show a response. We asked her about the possibility of brain damage if Deirdre should regain consciousness, but she said it was too soon to be worried about something like that. She reassured us to "just wait and see what happens here. You can never tell in these cases."

Our reaction to this development was not what we had expected it would be. We had waited so long for any type of change or responsiveness in Deirdre's physical condition, yet when this development presented itself, we reacted with mixed thoughts and emotions. If was difficult to shake the nagging feeling that with consciousness might come disability.

It was a thought everyone seemed to be having.

The Paradox of Release

The possibility of Deirdre's returning with a handicap caused more dissension than any other issue we had yet faced, and each of us had a different opinion as to what this might mean. We knew that many handicapped persons are advanced souls who had accepted their disability and come to earth for the purpose of teaching others. Could it be possible that Deirdre would return with a handicap for this purpose? There might be much to learn from that experience. Then again, did willingness to accept this possibility mean we were, in effect, giving up and saying that a miracle was no longer possible? And what about Deirdre's original life purpose? She had left her body to seek guidance about her life mission. Would a handicap prevent her from completing it? Were we betraying our faith by being willing to accept something less than what we knew was possible? Our consideration of these questions forced us to examine the complexities of the confusing paradox of release.

A Three-Step Process. At first glance "letting go and letting God" may seem to be passive, but it actually involves an active element. Release is a three-step process, wherein the third step may seem at odds with the first two, although a closer examination will show that this is not so. The third step is most important for it is the step which permits the process of release to move to the level of manifestation.

The first step in the release process is to acknowledge that "Thy will be done," thereby agreeing to align your will with God's will. You agree to accept whatever divine will wants, knowing that it wants only the highest good for all concerned. The second step is to release all expectation of how and when divine will may manifest. You agree to let go of your desire to control the situation and stop anticipating. The third step is actually an extension of the first. It requires that you hold to the absolute highest ideal of what you know God to be, and expect that ideal to manifest. It is perhaps the most critical step of the release process, for *thought equals vibration equals manifestation*. By holding the highest ideal or thought possible, you transmit that vibration into the universe and allow it to manifest in accordance with spiritual law.

Tino was the most vocal about expecting nothing less than a complete and total recovery because he was holding true to the highest ideal of what he believed God to be—all-knowing and all-good. If God's love never wants less than the best for us, why should we? He felt that if we were willing to expect less than that, we were doubting God's ability to create the miracle. If we were willing to have Deirdre back "at any cost," as some of us were, we were seeing through a limited, human perspective. A willingness to settle for less than we knew was possible would limit our options, restrict possible outcomes, and in effect be "bargaining" with God. We were actually trying to control the situation by dictating the likelihood of certain outcomes and negatively influencing the process of manifestation.

We had to learn to see from a divine perspective and know that, with God, all things are possible. By holding fast to the highest ideal we knew possible, we would know that we had done all we could to bring that ideal into manifestation and thus be able to accept any outcome, trusting the infinite wisdom of Spirit to bring about that which would be for the highest good of all concerned. If we were willing to accept a disability and a disability manifested, we would forever wonder if our lack of vision had dictated that outcome. If, however, we expected a miracle, we would be assured that whatever outcome might be manifested, it would be for the greatest good.

Convinced of the need to visualize our highest ideal, Tino went to speak with Deirdre. Acknowledging that the decision to return was hers, he told her that if she chose to return, she could return whole and healthy. A complete miracle was possible and we would continue to expect nothing less. With this simple utterance, Tino completed the third step of release and carried us along with him. He let go and let God-power do its work, through the power of the spoken word.

THE POWER OF THE SPOKEN WORD

The spoken word is the prime organizational vibration of conscious thought. It is a vehicle of creative power that gives form and expression to ideas. Words form a matrix of vibration and enable thought to manifest in physical form and action. Mark Twain, a master of words himself, remarked on this power:

> "A powerful agent is the right word. Whenever we come upon one of those intensely right words . . . the resulting effect is physical as well as spiritual, and electrically prompt." [9]

Ethnographic studies have shown that the language of a culture has a profound effect on that culture's experience of reality. The power of words to motivate people to action has been recognized for centuries, and history has shown that the most successful leaders are those who mastered the persuasive power of speech. The writers of the Declaration of Independence changed the direction of this country through the words they put to paper. Winston Churchill mobilized an entire nation to action through his eloquent use of words. Practitioners of the Japanese martial arts know that a "*kiai*," a cry uttered in a minor key, has the power to effect partial paralysis in one's opponent by abruptly lowering the arterial blood pressure. Even the biblical account of creation indicates that the universe began with an idea which was willed into creation through sound: "In the beginning was the Word . . . " (John 1:1)

In short, words spoken aloud not only create emotions,

but they also create action; therefore, they can shape our destiny. Indeed, Tino's words were to have a profound effect on the events that followed.

A Puzzling Change

Although none of us knew of Tino's conversation with Deirdre, it was shortly after this that we all detected a change of some kind. It was difficult to pinpoint at first, but it seemed as if there had been a change in Deirdre's "spiritual" presence.

For the past five days, we had always been able to sense that Deirdre's soul-self was nearby. Even when she was in the "coaching session," we could feel that she was in close proximity. Now, however, it was as if no one could detect her presence. "Something" had changed. Deirdre had gone.

Although we all sensed this difference, there was no corresponding change in her physical condition. In fact, her condition had improved slightly as the doctors were now detecting a pupil response in both eyes. Needless to say, we were confused by this turn of events and didn't understand what was happening. The physical signs indicated that she was getting stronger. Yet we were certain that Deirdre had left, but where or why she had gone we did not know.

Temple Meditations

The dinner hour was usually a slow time for us as the visitors who continued to call throughout the day usually tapered off at this period. Today was no different, and we decided to use this break to meditate. We hoped that we might learn something that would help us understand where Deirdre had gone. Brenda, Sharon, Dot, Bill, and Tino were there and we each entered into meditation.

During my meditation, I found myself in a temple of some sort. I was in a circular-shaped room with an ex-

tremely high ceiling and many windows which looked out
on a plush landscape. The room seemed to be bathed in a
beautiful light of many colors. The room had several doors
which I knew led to other areas. I noticed a large mirror
hanging on one wall. In the center of the room was a high
table surrounded by a step-like railing. On top of the table, I
thought I saw a large book. I didn't see anyone while I was
there, but I knew that people came there to read the book.

Although each of our meditations was different, several
did share common elements, such as large rooms, bright
lights, colorful crystals, and books. After hearing about our
experiences, Bill believed that he knew where we had gone.
He was certain that his meditation had led him to the Hall
of Akashic Records, and he believed that all our meditations
were but differing perceptions of that same place.

The Akashic Records.   The akashic records are sometimes called the "Book of Remembrance" or the "Book of
Life." They are the records of each soul's total experience.
Each entity's thoughts, emotions, and actions, both during
and between earthly sojourns, are recorded on the "skein of
time and space" and stored in this repository which thus
contains all knowledge of the Universal Mind. Cayce described the records as a type of library, where all knowledge,
including information on future possibilities, could be ac-
cessed and previewed.[10] Review of your record can help you
come to a better understanding of your true self and your
relationship to the Creative Forces and to better comprehend your purpose and experiences in the material plane.
Anyone, however, may access these records and thereby
gain the knowledge contained therein. Cayce reviewed the
akashic records when he gave his readings, and other
psychics have been reported to possess this ability.

The similarities in our meditations led us to believe that
Deirdre had gone to this Hall of Records. As we discussed
possible reasons for this, Tino told us about his conversation with Deirdre. Once we learned about it, things began

to fall into place. Perhaps Deirdre had been planning to return with a handicap and Tino's words caused her to reconsider this course. Perhaps she was contemplating other courses of action and needed to know what their ramifications might be. Perhaps she had gone to the records to retrieve information on how to effect a complete healing. Or, perhaps she had to see if she could complete her original life mission. Another possibility was that by finally fitting all the puzzle pieces together so that a miracle *was* possible, we opened the door to an unexpected option. Perhaps she had to visit the records to gain insight into this development.

Whatever the reason, Deirdre had gone to access information contained in the akashic records, information which most likely concerned her life path. It did not appear that she had stayed long, however, and we were still unable to locate where she had gone.

CALL HER HOME

It was Mary who provided some insight into where Deirdre might be. She reminded us that she was only a ten-year-old child, a little girl, who had been through a tremendous amount of experiences within the last few days. Mary had the distinct feeling that she had gone off to play, totally unaware of the turmoil her departure had caused. Mary believed it was time to call her home.

As soon as Mary spoke, I knew she was right, and a picture came into my mind. I could see Deirdre playing on a beach. She was holding a baby (perhaps Morgan?) in one arm and had a little boy (Matthew?) by the hand. I thought I saw a dog playing at her feet. They seemed to be playing with the waves and chasing seagulls. How appropriate, I thought, that Deirdre would be off playing by the ocean. When I was stationed in the New England area, we often spent time at the beach, where Deirdre's greatest joy had been to chase the seagulls as they landed close by.

Yes, it was likely that Deirdre had gone off to play, unmindful of the chaos this had caused. She was, after all, just a little girl, and she needed to be reminded that it was time to come home. As we continued our bedside vigil, we spoke out loud and told her that playtime was over. It was time to come back home.

THE DARK ABYSS

Our path up the mountain was reaching ever nearer to the summit, but first we had to cross the most critical segment of our journey. The rocks strewn across our path gave way to boulders which, at times, seemed to completely block our way. Footing became treacherous as sheer rock replaced worn trails. Ahead of us, the path wound its way into a dark cave where light disappeared and we came face to face with our greatest fears. Deep into the cave the path abruptly stopped, cut through by a wide, deep chasm. For a time we stood motionless, and it appeared there was no way across.

Slowly, through the murky shadows, a dim light became visible overhead, and we could see a sheer rock face rising high above the chasm. It appeared that our only way out was to go upward. The only way around the chasm was to conquer our fears and begin the arduous climb up the cliff before us. Footing and hand holds were slippery; a wrong choice meant a fall to certain death, and we realized that there was no way humanly possible to scale this rock. Had we come this far only to fall short of our destination? There was nothing we could do except to hold on to one another in love. In a final act of sheer desperation, we called out and relinquished our fate into the hands of a Higher Power. By doing so, we opened the door that allowed the Universal Spirit to reach down in love and pull us through.

✳ ✳ ✳

Let us not forget that such service [to others] is never lost, for with love it has been woven into the souls of those for whom we worked. It will shine forth again and again in the lives of many yet unborn. Love never dies; it is eternal.
—A Search for God, *Book I,* p. 126

PART II

———————

FROM CRISIS
TO MIRACLE

7

Jump Start to Consciousness

The Third Insight would lead us to believe that the universe, at its core, is like a kind of pure energy that is malleable to human intention and expectation, as though our expectation itself causes our energy to flow out into the world and affect other energy systems.

—The Celestine Prophecy

WE continued to "call Deirdre home" during our long vigils of Wednesday night. Her physical condition remained stable and her pupils showed an increasing response to light. In some ways, this turn of events was even more frustrating for us. She seemed poised on the brink of recovery and yet she was still so far away. By morning, slight eye movement could be detected, although there were no signs of consciousness.

Brad returned early Thursday and once again channeled energy as he had done the day before. After he finished, it was obvious that this was taking a heavy toll on him as well. While at work yesterday, he had continued to mentally send energy to Deirdre. Now this second "hands-on" energy transfer had left him even more drained. We had never seen Brad tired before, let alone exhausted.

It seemed that all of us were suffering some kind of physical ailment. Bill eventually required bed rest because of his flu symptoms. Brenda and I required prescription medication to treat severe coughs, and the others had succumbed to the common cold. The strain of the last week had taken its toll, and our attempts to work with energy had played havoc with our health. It was obvious that we had a lot to learn.

Prayer Continues

In this, the sixth day of our ordeal, we recognized more than ever the need for constant prayer and continued to rely on the support of the prayer network that had grown around us. Our family and friends, in turn, continued to hold us in love and prayer.

At my navy command, Thursday marked the occurrence of the weekly all-hands meeting called "quarters." I received a call that morning and learned that even there, in the midst of a busy military organization, there was time for prayer.

It seemed that there had been several requests from command members to hold a brief prayer session during quarters. As Nancy put it, "I told them that all you had asked for from the command was prayer, and the least they could do was allow a few minutes of silence so those of us who wanted to could pray." Much to everyone's surprise, the captain agreed, and quarters began with a few moments of prayer for Deirdre.

As I returned to the waiting room following the phone

call from Nancy, I mused on the fact that a week before, no one would have believed that this command, beset by an unusual number of internal conflicts, could have pulled together and joined in the common purpose of prayer. I was just beginning to grasp some idea of the far-reaching effects our experience was having on others.

First Awakenings

By mid-morning, it was apparent that Deirdre's physical condition was changing. Rapid eye movement beneath her eyelids had become more demonstrable and everyone felt an unexplainable excitement that something was about to occur.

As to what occurred first, I am not entirely sure, but by Thursday afternoon, several people had witnessed both head movement and movement in her right hand. Deirdre was struggling to regain consciousness!

Just as the onset of this disease had hit quickly and without warning, so, too, did the first indications of recovery progress in a rapid manner. Within hours, the finger movement of the right hand developed into an ability to grasp and hold on to our fingers. The head movement became more definite and seemed to occur in response to verbal cues. By evening, Deirdre was able to squeeze with both her right *and* her left hand, and nod her head in response to our voices.

Realizing that she was fighting her way back to consciousness, we intensified our efforts at sending healing energy and strength to her body. We also maintained a constant vigil, talking incessantly about what had happened during the last week. We knew that when she awoke, she would most likely be confused and frightened. We wanted to reassure her by explaining what had happened.

By evening, there was no doubt that Deirdre was nodding her head and squeezing her hand in response to our prompting. We asked her if she could open her eyes and, with what seemed great effort, she managed to open them slightly. She seemed so weak, so frail. We told her to save her strength and keep her eyes closed until she was stronger.

This was not an easy process by any means. Each movement seemed like a task that required a gargantuan effort on Deirdre's part. Each nod was a labor in agony; each hand squeeze, a taxing endeavor. The remorse I felt at remembering how I had scolded her for being weak and unable to accept pain gripped me once again. Now here she was, fighting against an incredible affliction which would reduce even the strongest individuals to their knees, mustering all her inner strength in order to heal her body and return to us.

I knew that as each breath brought her closer to consciousness, it also brought a greater awareness of physical pain. She had a growing awareness of the respirator tube down her throat, the feeding tube in her nose, the i.v.'s, tubes and needles that riddled her body, and the bolt protruding from her forehead. This awareness was just beginning to translate into sensations of pain. Each short period of responsiveness was followed by hours of deep, coma-like sleep. But despite the pain that consciousness would bring, we rejoiced that we had finally reached the turning point, and we believed that it would only be a matter of time before Deirdre regained full consciousness.

The struggle was far from over, however, for it was still too early to tell if there would be any residual effects from the disease. Although the staff had rescinded the "Do Not Revive" order, they continued to warn us about the likelihood of brain damage and paralysis, pointing out that Deirdre had yet to move her legs and feet. As always, however, we put our hope and faith in the miracle-working ability of a power greater than ourselves. We had come further than anyone had expected, and we were certainly not going to give up now.

HEALING FOR OTHERS

By Thursday evening, there was a perceptible shift in the feelings and attitudes of the pediatric ICU staff. The nurse's chair which had been moved away two days ago had been moved back next to Deirdre's bed. A rocking chair appeared for our use, so that we could sit in some comfort while we watched Deirdre. The nurses were talking among themselves and asking us questions about what we had been doing with Deirdre. Quiet conversations with words like "amazing," "unbelievable," and, yes, even "miracle" became commonplace. Even the families with whom we shared the waiting room were affected. Morgan's parents told us they had found new hope, because they felt that if Deirdre could recover, their own daughter might have a chance also.

It was Janet, Matthew's mother, who had the greatest reaction. We had talked to her frequently over the course of the last several days, as she questioned us about our actions. We had, of course, shared information and ideas with her, although she seemed skeptical that our efforts would achieve results. Now, however, people were beginning to realize that our actions *had* made a difference. That evening, a chair was placed next to Matthew's bed, and his grandmother sat in it as she held her grandson, talked to him, and massaged his arms and legs. It wasn't long before several of the nurses were also treating Matthew in this manner. It seemed as though the nursing staff was beginning to adopt our methods and apply them to other children in the ICU.

SHE'S RESPONDING!

The medical personnel who attended Deirdre on Wednesday and Thursday were keenly aware of her progress and made every attempt to encourage her and to watch for further indications of improvement. There were some doctors and nurses, however, who had not been on duty since Tuesday, when the prognosis had been very different. When they returned, their disbelief was evident. It was almost as if they could not accept the possibility of recovery. In fact, when Dr. Chaves returned on Friday and was briefed by Dr. Pardo on Deirdre's recovery, he told her, "I won't believe it until I see her walking and talking."

One doctor who fell into the skeptic category came on duty shortly after midnight Thursday. Darcie was with Deirdre at the time, and she gave us this account of the incident.

Without reviewing Deirdre's chart, the doctor checked the monitors and immediately called the nurse.

"I don't like this number," he said. "It doesn't make sense."

The nurse responded, "Really, doctor, I don't think there's any need for concern now."

"Have you noticed anything else unusual?" he continued.

"No, doctor, everything else is fine."

"But, I'm concerned about this number!" he repeated.

Somewhat exasperated the nurse responded, "But, doctor, she's responding so well!"

"Responding?" he questioned, looking up from his papers. "What do you mean she's responding?"

"Deirdre has been responsive since this morning," the nurse replied again. "Check her chart!"

Darcie interjected at this point.

"Deirdre," she said, "show the doctor you can nod your head." Deirdre nodded.

"Now squeeze the doctor's hand for me." As the doctor reached out his hand, Deirdre responded by grasping it with hers.

"And, Deirdre," Darcie continued, "do you think you can open your eyes for the doctor?" Again, with great effort, Deirdre managed to crack open her eyelids for a second or two.

"You see, doctor?" the nurse added. "I told you she was responding."

The doctor stood there for a moment in disbelief. He had been so preoccupied with his own expectations that he had never considered the possibility that there might have been a favorable change in Deirdre's condition. He was so sure about what he thought must happen that he hadn't even bothered to check her chart.

"I, I can't believe it," he stuttered. "She's responding? *She's responding!*" he shouted. "Oh my God, this is *incredible.* I can't believe this. I just can't believe it. I have to go tell them. They won't believe it either."

Without any further explanation, this doctor literally ran out of the room and down the hall shouting, *"She's responding!"* Who "they" were, I don't know. I assume "they" were staff members in another department. But I do know that he cut quite a figure jumping, dancing, and shouting, as he raced through the halls after midnight.

PHONE HOME

I was awakened in the waiting room Friday morning by Brenda and Darcie, who told me that I must go and see Deirdre at once.

"Is something wrong?" I asked.

No, there wasn't anything wrong. They just wanted me to see Deirdre nod her head and squeeze my hand.

"She was doing that yesterday," I told them.

"Not like *this*," Brenda responded, a big smile on her face. "Now she's *really* doing it!"

When I saw Deirdre, I knew what they meant. I called her name and she vigorously nodded her head up and down several times. Then I put my hand by hers and she grabbed my thumb and squeezed so hard I thought it might break. It was the best thing I had ever felt.

"Go ahead," I told her. "You can squeeze my thumb as

hard as you want. I don't even care if you break it!"

Her response was to squeeze it even harder a second time.

"Now, Deirdre," Brenda said. "Open your eyes for your mom."

Slowly, ever so slowly it seemed, Deirdre's eyelids pried open. There for the first time in a week, I saw my daughter looking back at me through her deep brown eyes. She was back. I couldn't help but start to cry.

My crying seemed to upset Deirdre so I tried to explain that I was crying because I was so happy. She had come back to us. That's all that mattered. Then I sat and talked with her, telling her again about everything that had happened in the last seven days.

As I talked to her, she moved my fingers so that they touched the small "cap" on one of her fingers. This finger cap monitored her pulse and was connected by wire to one of the monitors. Although she didn't realize it, the cap contained a small light, which glowed continuously so that it could be easily seen in the dark. I surmised that she was curious about this strange device connected to her finger.

I explained what it was and she nodded. I told her it reminded me of the movie character "ET" 's *(The Extraterrestrial)* finger because it glowed like his did. Then I told her that many, many times a day, I had come and held her hand and asked her to "phone home," as "ET" had tried to do.

"*Phone home,* Deirdre," I had said. "Just like 'ET,' please *phone home.* Let us know how you are."

Suddenly, Deirdre's countenance changed and I realized that she was starting to cry. Holding her tight, I told her there was no need for tears. After all, she *had* phoned home.

Words of Caution

Despite the improvements in Deirdre's condition, the doctors continued to warn us not to be too optimistic about her recovery. While it was apparent that she would live, they still had serious doubts as to the completeness of her recovery. The initial concerns regarding possible paralysis rapidly diminished, however, as she began to wiggle her toes Friday afternoon. This was a great relief to us, because her feet had been an area of concern. Once her toes began to wiggle, we knew it wouldn't be long before she would regain complete movement in both legs.

While the concerns about Deirdre's physical recovery began to lessen, the doubts about her mental recovery remained. The doctors continued to warn us that it was quite possible she would have severe memory loss along with some degree of mental retardation. They felt they would have a more accurate prognosis if and when she began to talk.

First Words

Talk, I thought, how could she talk? She was still connected to the respirator. How could she talk with that hose blocking her throat? Again, however, Deirdre was going to surprise us all.

Lucid Thought. Friday afternoon as I was talking to Deirdre, I mentioned that Operation Desert Storm was over. When I told her that the war was over and we had won, she gave me a puzzling look, and only then did I realize how strange it must have seemed to her. When she first became ill, the conflict was in full swing. Now, although a week had passed, she had no conscious memory of those days. What had been a week to us seemed like only minutes to her.

Then Deirdre reached up with her hand and pulled me close. With my ear near her mouth, I realized that she was trying to speak despite the respirator tube in her throat. Leaning closer, I made out the following sound:

"*Beej.*" She looked at me hopefully.

"*Beej,*" I repeated.

"Bee-jguh," she managed again.

I was stumped. What could "bee-jguh" possibly mean? And what did it have to do with the war? I searched for some association between this word and the war, and after a few minutes I finally made the connection. Deirdre was trying to say "B. J." B.J. was her cousin, who had recently joined the navy. He was at boot camp when Operation Desert Storm began and she was very worried that he would have to go and fight. Now, since I had told her the war was over, she was asking about B.J!

"B.J.," I queried. "You want to know about your cousin B.J.?"

Deirdre nodded yes.

"B.J. will be fine," I told her. "Since the war is over, he won't have to go fight."

I thought I detected a sigh of relief.

"Were you asking me that since the war is over, B.J. wouldn't have to go fight?"

Again she nodded. In that instant, I knew that Deirdre's thinking processes would be all right. She had not only remembered B.J., but she had made a connection between the end of the war and his situation. She could still make logical deductions!

When I told Dr. Pardo about this a few hours later, she indicated that it was a very good sign indeed.

Footprints.   Later that afternoon, I asked Deirdre if she would like me to tell her a story. Pulling me close, she tried to speak again. I held my ear to her mouth and tried to understand her words.

"Fut-prinz."

"Footprints? The poem *Footprints?"* I asked with surprise. She nodded yes.

Deirdre had never indicated any particular interest in this poem before, so I was quite surprised when she asked to hear it. To the best of my ability, I recalled the story of the man who had a dream that he was walking along a beach with the Lord. As they walked, he was shown the scenes of his life. In each scene, there were two sets of footprints: one his and one belonging to the Lord. After the last scene had played, he looked back and saw that at the worst times of his life there was only one set of footprints. Troubled by this, he asked the Lord why He had left him alone at those times. The Lord answered that He had never left him. Instead, it was during those times of trial and suffering that the Lord had carried him.

As I recited this tale and tears ran down Deirdre's face, I began to wonder about the significance of this request. But before I could think further, Deirdre pulled me close and asked for a second story.

Angel Rescue. As I listened to her words, I could not understand them. I could make out four syllables but the words were garbled. My mind raced trying to make sense of the sounds.

"Bah-en-en-snek."

Useless. I repeated several variations on the combination of sounds, to no avail. Deirdre was becoming frustrated. I knew it pained her to talk, but I just couldn't make out the words. She tried again.

This time I understood the first word as "boy." "Boy-en-a," but I still couldn't make out that last word. What story did I know that had to do with a boy and something starting with the letter "s"? I couldn't recall any stories that fit that description. Yet, if she were asking for it, I must know it. I racked my brain trying to remember.

Then out of the blue, I remembered that several months before I had read an article in *Reader's Digest* about a boy who had been bitten by a snake! That was it! That was the story! The details came rushing back to memory as I talked about the boy bitten by a snake. Unconscious in a rural area, he somehow appeared on the front porch of a distant cabin where he was found and rushed to a hospital. Authorities could not understand how the boy, unconscious and with a leg swollen three times its normal size, had been able to drag himself over a half mile of wooded terrain. After recovering from a weeklong near-death coma, the boy told astonished family members that he had been carried by an angel. The angel had told him he needed to go away for a little while, to heal completely, before returning to his family.

I didn't even think that Deirdre had paid much attention to this story when I had told her about it a few months ago, and yet now it was one of her first requests upon regaining consciousness. A boy in a near-death coma carried by an angel, and a man carried by the Lord in times of trouble. These were the thoughts on Deirdre's mind only a few hours after waking up from a weeklong coma, and they were certainly not the questions I had expected. I was stunned by her interest in such esoteric issues so soon after regaining consciousness, and shivers ran up and down my spine as I pondered the implications of these requests.

Discussing this with the others, we could only guess the significance of Deirdre's request to hear these stories so soon after regaining consciousness. Was she, perhaps, seeking confirmation of her own remembrances while in the coma? Or perhaps this was her way of letting us know what she did remember? We felt that the most plausible explanation was a combination of the two. We knew that angels had surrounded us all, and we felt certain that Deirdre had been in their presence as well. We certainly believed that Jesus had been with her the entire time. On some level, we concluded, Deirdre must have a memory of what happened to her during her out-of-body sojourn.

A Few Steps More

By now we felt that we were nearing the end of our journey. We had traveled a great distance and learned much in the process, but the journey was far from over. There was one last hill to climb, a few final lessons to be learned. We knew, however, that the end of the trail lay just beyond our sight, obscured only by a few wisps of clouds. We could not lose our footing so near to our goal. Now more than ever it was vitally important to keep our eyes fixed on the path before us and not be deterred from reaching the summit.

* * *

Medical science is starting to accept that it has something important to learn from the near-death experiences of children ... Comatose patients ... may actually be undergoing a profound experience that involves total awareness of what is going on around them ... We need to acknowledge the healing power of a near-death experience.
—Melvin Morse, M.D., *Closer to the Light*

8

Return to Wellness

To picture health is one of the most scientific ways of producing it in the body. To picture health is also one of the quickest roads to healing.
— Catherine Ponder, *The Dynamic Laws of Healing*

Recovery Begins

WE greeted the advent of the second weekend of our ordeal with a sense of joy and thanksgiving. Each hour seemed to bring Deirdre another step closer to recovery. Several of the arterial catheters had been disconnected and late Saturday morning she underwent minor surgery to remove the cranial bolt; all traces of brain swelling had dissipated, and it was no longer necessary to monitor cranial pressure. A few stitches were all that remained to remind us of the cranial trauma Deirdre had endured.

Physically, Deirdre was still very weak, although this was understandable because of her prolonged inactivity caused by the coma. Muscles normally used in simple, everyday activities had already begun to atrophy in the short span of a week. She tired quickly and spent a great deal of time sleeping to regain her strength. Concerned about the weakened condition of her lungs, the doctors felt it would be best to keep her on the respirator for a few days more. She was still being fed through the nasal feeding tube and it would be some time before she would be weaned from that. And of course, as with any ICU patient, she was still connected to an i.v. Yet despite these limiting conditions, it was very apparent that her physical condition was growing stronger with each passing day.

Mentally, Deirdre had lost a week of her life. She had no conscious memory of what had happened during the last seven days, and she looked at us in amazement when we described the events that had occurred. The visitors, the prayers, the many things we had experienced no doubt sounded incredible.

To cheer her, we showed her the many cards we had received and the cards written by her classmates that Jenny had brought. The mention of Jenny brought tears to her eyes and she softly repeated "*Jenny?*" I told her that yes, Jenny had come to see her and was very sorry about the fight they had. She gingerly touched the card Jenny made, and I assured her that Jenny would be back to visit when she was stronger.

Deirdre's mental comprehension and alertness continued to show improvement. The respirator, however, still made it difficult for her to talk, and we had to find other ways to communicate. Primarily, we would ask her "yes and no" questions to which she would respond with a hand squeeze or head nod. The lucidity of her responses indicated that she was regaining use of her mental faculties. As with her physical condition, her mental clarity improved daily.

ALLAYING FEARS

Dealing with the nuances of Deirdre's recovery presented a new set of problems and challenges. These stemmed not only from the physical pain that waking consciousness brought, but from the feelings of fear she was experiencing. The respirator tube caused a burning sensation in her mouth and throat, and the i.v. needles hurt her wrists. The arterial catheters caused her the most pain, and she said that each time she moved it felt as if they were digging into her thighs and ripping her skin. Yet even worse than the physical pain was the sense of fear she felt as she began to realize what had happened to her. After all, she was a very scared and confused little girl, who really didn't understand what had taken place. All she knew was that she had gone to sleep in her bed and awoke a week later in a hospital, with needles and tubes stuck into her body and people gathering around her saying it was a miracle that she was alive. That would certainly be a heavy load for any adult to accept, let alone a ten-year-old child!

A great deal of our time was, therefore, spent in trying to explain what had happened, addressing her fears and concerns, and reassuring her that, despite it all, everything *was* going to be all right. We had to reassure her that the pain was temporary and that her fears would subside. We wanted her to know that a complete recovery *was* possible and help her visualize that outcome. We told her of the many people who continued to pray for her and encouraged her to draw upon the healing energy their prayers had generated.

The Strength of the Group. The first few days of Deirdre's waking consciousness were more difficult than expected. It would take a group effort of continued prayer and meditation to get us through those difficult days. Even though we knew she was going to recover, it was hard to watch her lying there knowing that she was suffering. It was particularly hard on Tino, who felt that he should be able to do more for her. He wanted to take away the pain and not being able to do so made him feel helpless and angry.

I, on the other hand, had a different reaction. While Deirdre was comatose, I had to force myself to stay with her. Seeing my beautiful child lying cold and unresponsive was hard to bear. Once I knew she would recover, however, it was easier for me to accept the fact that she would have to endure some temporary pain. I also felt that, in some way, I could help her work through this difficult time.

Hidden Talents. When the pain became especially unbearable, I would hold Deirdre's hand and have her squeeze mine as hard as she could, telling her to think of the pain passing out through her hand and disappearing into mine. When her fears would become especially overwhelming, I would do the same and tell her that, as she cried, her tears would carry away the fear. Deirdre always seemed to feel better following these episodes, and Brenda felt that I had discovered a hidden talent, a talent which allowed me to teach Deirdre how to release her fear and pain.

Sharon also demonstrated an unknown talent. She had the ability to sit quietly with Deirdre and know exactly what she was thinking or what question she wanted to ask. Sharon would state the question that she *thought* Deirdre wanted to ask, and Deirdre would inevitably nod yes, this *was* her question. This talent proved very useful during the days when Deirdre was still connected to the respirator and unable to talk.

As she had throughout the past week, Brenda continued to be our guide and motivation, pulling together information, analyzing developments, and suggesting a continued plan of action. Dot, much to our surprise, turned out to be our strength during the night, as she spent many past-midnight hours with Deirdre, reassuring her with her quiet presence. Darcie, recovered from her own illness, lit up the ICU with her well-honed Irish wit and provided a needed sense of comic relief as she demonstrated the ability to make Deirdre laugh, even in the face of pain. Tino took care of many of the mundane issues that we needed to address. Mary continued to bless us with her uplifting visits. Brad returned to give Deirdre more energy. And although Bill had become quite ill with the flu and was recovering at home, he continued to hold us in near constant prayer. Joye and Jeanne continued to do the same.

As we had throughout this crisis, we still prayed and meditated, both individually and as a group. We discovered that we each had unique abilities and talents. We each had different strengths and weaknesses, and we learned to rely on one another. By cooperating together, we helped to make one another stronger and our journey a little less difficult.

THE MIRACLE SPREADS

This weekend would prove to be one that the staff of the pediatric ICU would not soon forget. Not only was Deirdre showing signs of a miraculous recovery, but she would be joined by two other children who would defy the odds and live: Matthew and Morgan.

By Saturday, Matthew had awakened and was showing amazing improvement! His seizures had stopped, his physical functions were returning to normal, and it was evident that he, too, was going to recover! For the second time in two days there was joy and elation in the ICU, and the staff was soon talking with wonder about a second miracle.

This atmosphere of hope and excitement intensified again late Sunday, when baby Morgan was held by her mother for the first time. I will always remember her mother returning to the waiting room, a look of joy and wonder on her face, as she described what it was like to hold her child.

Morgan was responding with unexpected and remarkable improvement, and her prognosis for recovery was good. A third miracle had begun.

By the end of the weekend, the staff seemed beside themselves with amazement! One miraculous recovery was understandable. After all, such things do happen. But three in so short a time? Particularly when these three children were part of a "prayer triad" being prayed for by a somewhat unusual group of people who did not hesitate to voice their belief in its power. It wasn't long before more than one nurse—and yes, even a few doctors—shared with us their beliefs that prayer can and does work miracles.

As we participated in these families' happiness, we said a prayer of thanks to God, to the Christ, to the many angels who watched over these children, and for the many people who were still actively taking part in the prayer network. For we knew that it was their prayers and their love that had helped make these miracles possible.

MARVELOUS MONOTONE

By Saturday night, the respirator was causing Deirdre a great deal of discomfort. It was a source of constant irritation and we pleaded that it be removed. Even the nurses on duty that night realized that it was more of a hindrance than a help and requested permission to remove it. One nurse said that she was tempted to just pull it out and report that Deirdre had pushed it out herself.

The hospital had rules, however, and the rules said that no one could be disconnected from a respirator unless a full staff was onboard, and a full staff would not be available until Sunday morning. So Deirdre spent a very restless night "fighting" with the respirator tube and imploring us to "*get it out*." We stood by feeling even more helpless and frustrated than usual.

Finally, mid-Sunday morning, our numerous pleas to the

doctors achieved results. With a full staff onboard, the respirator was disconnected and the tube removed while Deirdre slept. She had actually practiced breathing "around" the tube earlier, and she had no difficulty breathing on her own. As a precaution, however, she was given oxygen for another day, but this did not interfere with her ability to talk.

When Deirdre awoke and realized that the hated tube was gone, she immediately tried to speak. Hearing her talk for the first time was quite a shock for it seemed that her voice had changed. It was raspy and raw, of course, but more surprisingly, she spoke in a flat, level monotone devoid of all inflection or intonation. It would take another two weeks before her voice would return to normal. Yet that "robot-like" monotone was the most beautiful sound I have ever heard.

Disconnecting the respirator was a very important step in Deirdre's recovery. Dr. Pardo had indicated that once Deirdre had been off the respirator for twenty-four hours, they could consider a transfer out of pediatric ICU to the pediatric ward. If she continued to show improvement, she might be transferred as early as Monday or Tuesday. We greeted this news with jubilant expectation. It seemed as if we had spent a lifetime in that waiting room, and we were anxious to move on to the next step of Deirdre's recovery.

Release from ICU

Following Monday morning's routine examination, Dr. Pardo informed us that she was planning to transfer Deirdre to pediatrics as soon as a bed became available. The transfer could take place as early as this afternoon! We were ecstatic and began to make preparations to pack up our "campsite" in the waiting room.

By early afternoon, a nurse informed us that a bed had opened up and Deirdre would be moved within a few hours. Using the boxes Tino had brought, we began to gather up the belongings we had accumulated: cards and letters, plants and flowers, the picture of Deirdre that had stood on an end table, some books and inspirational literature, fresh changes of clothing, the sign with our name on it, doughnuts, pastries, snacks, sodas, and a great deal of food stored in the cooler a friend had brought. We folded up the cots, blankets, and pillows and took them to our car. We were ready and anxious to go.

When it came time to move Deirdre, she was transferred from her bed to a mobile bed and wheeled out of ICU. Brenda, Darcie, and I accompanied her and pointed out our "campsite" in the waiting room as we passed. The pediatric ward was actually in a different building, and we had to go through much of the main hospital building. As we passed through the corridors, I described for Deirdre the different areas of the hospital that I had come to know so well.

As we walked, the nurse exchanged amenities with us. She surprised us by asking Deirdre if she knew the nickname she had been given by the staff.

"Nickname?" Deirdre questioned.

"Yes," replied the nurse. "They call you 'The Miracle Kid.' "

The Miracle Kid, I thought to myself. If they only knew. But then again, perhaps they did.

The main building was connected to several other buildings by a series of tunnels, some underground and some above-ground passageways. The building to which we were going was joined by an above-ground corridor lined with many windows. As we passed through this corridor, Deirdre was able to look on the outside world for the first time since becoming ill. The sun was shining and the ground was covered with the new growth of spring.

As we looked outside, we could see a garden where the first shoots of spring bulbs were just beginning to break through the ground. It was a beautiful sight to behold, and I couldn't help but reflect on the symbology of this moment. Just as we had moved from the shadowy corridor of the ICU through this passageway of sunlight to view the first signs of new life that spring brings, so, too, had we emerged from our own dark winter into the light of a new day.

THE PEDIATRIC SCENE

The pediatric ward was very different from the usually somber atmosphere of the pediatric ICU. For one thing, there were many windows, whereas the ICU and waiting room had none. That alone made for a much different setting. As we entered the pediatric wing, it was evident there was also a great deal more activity, noise, and foot traffic. Children, some on foot and others in wheelchairs, their i.v.'s in tow, moved through the halls on their way to and from scheduled activities.

Most of the rooms were doubles, and Deirdre's was no exception. She would share this room with a roommate whom we would meet shortly. The nurse wheeled Deirdre over to the bed near the window, and we helped her transfer Deirdre to her new bed. It was an ample-sized room, with two large chairs which folded out into beds, two straight-backed chairs, two dressers, two tables, and two clothes lockers. There was a sink and mirror in the center of the room, and a door which led to a private toilet. As far as Deirdre was concerned, however, the best feature of this room was the television set mounted on the wall.

Regaining Control. As we started to unpack, we heard the buzzing noise of the remote controls in action. As Darcie described it, Deirdre immediately sought to take "control" of her new environment.

"Head went up. Head went down. Feet went up. Feet went down. TV went on. Channels went round."

This was a very healthy sign, for we knew that one of the most demoralizing factors of hospitalization is the loss of control felt by most patients. Anything that helps patients regain even a small measure of control over some aspect of their environment can help boost morale, raise spirits, and hasten the rate of recovery.

It wasn't long before Deirdre's new roommate appeared. Barbie was a ten-year-old girl hospitalized with a congenital heart problem. Both she and her mother were very friendly and were "old pros" at hospitalization. Barbie had had five operations before the age of eight. It didn't take long for Deirdre and Barbie to become friends.

THE LONG ROAD OF PHYSICAL THERAPY

Once settled, Deirdre began the long walk down the road of physical rehabilitation. The ravages of Reye's syndrome had left her weak and debilitated. A pinched nerve in her left eye was causing a drooping eyelid and double vision, a condition which would continue for several months. She had lost much muscle tone and had to regain a sense of hand, eye, and body coordination. Since she was unable to sit or stand on her own, she had to use a bedpan instead of the bathroom.

The nurses told us that we could help by encouraging Deirdre to sit up on her own and eventually to stand. In a day or two she might be strong enough to use a wheelchair and, a few days after that, be ready to take a few steps with assistance. In time she would begin the process of relearning to walk. We were anxious to help because we knew that the more help we could provide, the quicker she would recover and the sooner we would go home.

Gaining Mobility. Beginning Tuesday morning, we took turns helping Deirdre sit up on the edge of the bed. At first she was very dizzy and complained that the room wouldn't stop spinning. We told her that it was important for her to sit up as much as possible so that her circulation would return to normal. A sitting position would also help break up the fluid that had accumulated in her lungs. After several attempts, she became more comfortable with this movement.

I knew that Deirdre was somewhat displeased with herself for having to use a bedpan, and I felt I could use this to motivate her to attempt to walk to the bathroom. At first she resisted this idea and was very fearful about leaving her bed. By late afternoon, however, I had convinced her that she could walk the few steps while I supported her.

As I held her by the arm, she made a successful attempt to stand. I waited until the dizziness subsided and guided her into the bathroom. The success of this achievement, however, was marred by the pain she felt upon urination. The catheters had cut and scarred her, and it would take time for these wounds to heal. I told her to squeeze my hand as hard as she could and visualize the pain passing from her body to mine. For the next week, I (or Tino) had to repeat this procedure over and over again. It was the only way she could cope with the painful burning sensation.

After finishing, I guided Deirdre to the sink so that she could wash her hands. I had forgotten about the mirror over the sink and, before I realized it, Deirdre caught sight of her reflection. She stared in disbelief. Her weight loss was reflected in her face, and the stitches from the cranial bolt were clearly visible. Her cheeks were sunken and shallow, pale and without color. Her hair resembled a matted mess.

I saw the tears well up in her eyes as she touched her hair and then her check. I searched for words of encouragement and told her that considering all she had been through, she looked wonderful. The stitches would disappear, her hair could be washed, and she would regain her old look and color. Despite the shock of seeing herself like this, she nodded in agreement.

While washing Deirdre's hair may have seemed like a simple matter, it actually turned into a hearty challenge. What we thought would be a routine task turned into a monumental undertaking. Darcie, Brenda, and I took turns washing her hair and afterward it took nearly three hours for Brenda to work out the tangles and loosen each twisted strand. I had never had an aptitude for this sort of thing, and I was grateful to have Brenda's assistance. It was just another example of the continued importance of the group's support, as we required assistance to complete what once had been routine tasks.

A short time later, a nurse made her rounds and suggested that we begin to encourage Deirdre to sit up. When we told her that Deirdre had not only sat up, but had walked (with help) to the bathroom, she was elated.

"You mean she's walked already?" she said. "That's amazing. That's wonderful progress, just wonderful. Now we can get rid of that bedpan."

Freedom of Movement. Tuesday was also important because it marked the removal of the last major irritant, the nasal feeding tube. This tube had caused Deirdre a great deal of discomfort over the last three days, and her nose was bleeding from the constant friction it created. As with the respirator, it took several requests before the nurses received permission to remove it. As it came out, we were all amazed at its length. Deirdre began a liquid diet of Ensure®, broth, and juice. By the end of the week was able to eat soup and soft foods.

With the feeding tube gone, we were ready to have Deirdre move into a wheelchair so that we could take her around the hospital. Again, she was reluctant to attempt this feat, but the promise of a trip to the gift shop served as motivation. Brenda, Darcie, and I transferred the i.v. bag to the wheelchair and helped Deirdre in. She complained of light-headedness as we proceeded down the hall, and the elevator proved a challenge in itself, but by the time we were ready to return to the room, we knew it had been a successful outing.

Professional Therapy. As we continued our efforts to help Deirdre regain control of her movements, she was also undergoing other forms of therapy. A respiratory therapist made three visits each day and taught Deirdre how to use a

"bubble pipe," an exhaler designed to increase lung capac-
ity. A physical therapist also made three visits each day and
led Deirdre in hand-and-finger exercises as well as range of
motion exercises designed to build arm and leg strength.
Deirdre also worked with clay putty to help build finger and
hand strength. Each therapist seemed pleased with her
progress.

QUIET TIME

Despite our joy at the quick pace of Deirdre's recovery,
we knew that it was still important to continue the prayer
effort. Deirdre still had a long way to go to complete recovery. The prayer network was still very active, and we wanted
to continue in prayer and meditation as well. The intrusive
atmosphere of the pediatric ward, however, was not conducive to this, particularly in group form. So, at least once
per day, several of us would break away and go to the hospital chapel for a silent time of prayer or meditation. These
quiet moments helped us keep our perspective and stay
grounded and centered, allowed us to thank God for the
miracle He had worked, and enabled us to ask for continued guidance in the days that lay ahead.

A NEW ROOMMATE

At mid-week, Barbie's tests were complete and she was
discharged. Fortunately, this had not been a serious episode, and we bid her a fond farewell. The next day, Deirdre
received a new roommate, Carrie. While Deirdre and Barbie
had been the same age and had similar interests, Carrie was
seventeen. They got along fairly well for the most part, except when it came to the choice of television programs.
Deirdre preferred cartoons, while Carrie preferred talk
shows. With one television and two remote controls, the
channel switching went something like this:

Ducktales. Donahue. Ducktales. Donahue.
Oprah. Gummi Bears. Oprah. Gummi Bears.

And so on. Fortunately, much of this was done with a sense of humor behind it and was not meant seriously. I viewed this behavior as a positive sign that Deirdre was regaining her strength and taking an active interest in things again.

VISITORS ON PARADE

While the new room was comfortable, it was not designed to accommodate more than a few people at a time. Tino, Brenda, Darcie, and I were there each day, sometimes joined by Dot. Sharon and Sara would join us in the evenings. Add to this visits from Brad, Jeanne, and our many other visitors, and we always had a full house. In the evenings we would often have several visitors at one time and would have to "overflow" into the sitting room or playroom.

Many of the people who had called while Deirdre was in ICU returned to visit her in pediatrics. Deirdre, of course, did not remember anything that had happened that first week, and she was amazed to learn that she'd had so many visitors. Friends and co-workers returned. Mrs. Kramer, the school nurse, came to call, her Sunday school teacher Mary came a second time, and even our hairdresser Trisha paid a second visit. Tom Abate made several visits and smuggled in candy bars. Mrs. Witte, Deirdre's fifth-grade teacher, arrived with a banner signed by classmates and faculty members. A second banner was given to her by Tino's friends and co-workers.

While Deirdre knew many of her visitors, there was an equal number of people whom she did not know. We introduced her to our friends whom she had known by name, but had never actually met. There were others, however, such as those we ourselves had first met that week, who were total strangers.

Compounding her confusion was the fact that so many people greeted her with a similar salutation:

"Deirdre, we love you. We prayed for you. It's a miracle!"

I could see that this exclamation often left her even more puzzled as she failed to recognize the person who had "loved and prayed for her." Sometimes, she would respond with a question of her own: "*Who are you?*" Many times, these visits were taxing and we had to keep them short. Deirdre still had a long way to go before she regained her normal strength and stamina.

Gifts Galore.   Each visitor, it seemed, showed up with a gift of some sort. Some brought cards or flowers, others brought plants, a few brought balloons, and many, many brought stuffed toys. Add to this the flowers, plants, and toys wired to us by friends, relatives, and yes, even strangers who had become involved in the prayer network, and it wasn't long before our side of the room looked more like a gift shop than a hospital room. Our quarters were becoming more crowded with each passing day, until even the nurses were making comments about the unusual number of gifts.

"Well, what do you expect?" one nurse commented. "After all, she is 'The Miracle Kid.' "

And while I wondered where we were going to find room for everything, Deirdre didn't seem to mind one bit.

A Friend Returns.   There was one visit which held a very special meaning for Deirdre. Late Tuesday afternoon, Jenny and her mother Carol returned for a second time. When Jenny and Deirdre saw one another, they each froze, their eyes locked. Without saying a word, both began to cry silent tears. I knew it was important for them to be alone, so I asked our other visitors to move to the sitting room. As we left, I saw Jenny leaning over the bed and hug Deirdre as they both continued to cry. I wasn't concerned, however, because I knew that this was a cleansing cry and marked the beginning of yet another healing process.

The Healing Power of a Baby.   Another visit of special

significance was the return of Tom, Lorna, and their infant son Iain. While Deirdre did not remember their first visit, she did remember Iain from the time she had seen him in the hospital nursery after he was born. The sight of Iain made her face light up and she asked Lorna, in her droll monotone, if she could bring him closer. Instead of just bringing him closer, however, Lorna handed Iain to Deirdre so that she could hold him. The look on Deirdre's face as she held that baby was truly radiant. She looked so happy and fulfilled.

"Look, Momma. She let me hold him."

Hearing those words, I realized that the simple act of holding this baby signified to her that we believed she was capable of caring for another and was, in essence, proof for her that she was getting well.

Surprise Visit. Perhaps our most surprising visitor was Joye, the one member of our study group whom we had advised not to come to the hospital because of her hypersensitive, empathic nature. Joye showed up one afternoon without warning, and we were all surprised to see her. Everyone except Deirdre, that is. Deirdre had asked about Joye less than an hour before she arrived. It was almost as if she had been expecting her. Joye's empathic nature made her susceptible to the feelings and emotions of others, and visits to places such as hospitals usually left her physically and emotionally drained. Yet for some reason, Joye felt compelled to come and see Deirdre. She said that she was a part of this miracle and wasn't going to miss out on the best part of it. Fortunately, she did not suffer any ill effects from that visit.

FEARFUL NIGHTS

Although our days in pediatrics were filled with visitors and other activities, our nights were a different story. Most of the visitors were gone by 9:00 p.m., and our fellow study group members departed by 10:00. UKMC permitted one parent to stay overnight with each child. The large easy chair converted into a single bed, and parents were supplied with a pillow and blanket. The first two nights, both Tino and I stayed with Deirdre, with Tino sleeping in another chair. Wednesday night, however, a new nurse told us that only one of us could be permitted to stay, and from that point on Tino and I alternated nightly stays.

The night seemed to be an especially hard time for Deirdre. She was reluctant to fall asleep, fearful that she would lapse back into a coma. In fact, she refused to sleep unless we held her hand. Once asleep, she frequently had bad dreams and would wake up screaming in pain and fear. She also had frequent coughing spells due to the fluid in her lungs. We had to reassure her that the worst of this experience was over and that she was going to be all right.

Yet even I still faced demons at night, fighting to overcome fears that she would have a relapse of some sort. Following one particularly bad coughing spell, I couldn't shake the irrational fear that she was going to stop breathing. I lay awake for hours as the fear gripped my heart. Yet I knew I couldn't let Deirdre see my fear, and I tried to maintain a positive focus for her sake. It was only through prayer, however, that I could bring that irrational fear under control.

The waking hour was not much better than the darkness, for it meant a visit by the nurse who routinely drew blood samples from each patient. Each morning she would appear before 6:00 a.m., and each morning Deirdre would scream in terror as, once again, the razor-sharp needles pricked her skin. Like me, Deirdre has "rolling veins" which make blood draws extremely difficult, and it often takes three or four sticks before a vein is hit. Tino and I had to help restrain her. And even though we understood that the procedure was necessary, we still hated it.

LEARNING TO WALK

Toward the end of the week, Deirdre had progressed to the point of being able to walk the length of the hall, with support. She was even able to take a few, halting steps without assistance. The medical staff continued to express amazement at the rapid rate of her recovery. Progress they thought might take weeks was being accomplished in a matter of days. Deirdre's hard work and our encouragement were making for a rapid recovery.

By the weekend, we were encouraging Deirdre to walk the length of the hall, from her room to the nurses' desk, *without assistance.* She had tried it before, but usually got no more than a few steps before stopping and calling for help. She was making another attempt and seemed ready to give up again when Dr. Brenda Stein, a resident in pediatrics, appeared at the other end of the hall. When she realized what we were doing, she did a most amazing thing. There, in front of the nurses' desk, she performed a cheerleading routine.

"Come on, Deirdre. Let's go, Deirdre. Give me a 'D' for do. Give me an 'E' for effort. Give me an 'I' for I can... " she shouted, accompanying her words with cheerleading motions.

I don't know who was more surprised—me, Deirdre, or the nurses. Dr. Stein had never struck me as the kind of person to do something so impetuous. She was always very professional and businesslike, seldom making small talk, and rarely asking personal questions. Although I knew she was a competent doctor, I had not been overly impressed by her bedside manner. Yet, here she was, going above and beyond the call of duty to provide Deirdre with just the motivation she needed. Responding to Dr. Stein's cheers, Deirdre began to walk hesitantly and then more surely until she strode triumphantly to her side. I realized with regret that I had misjudged Dr. Stein and thanked her profusely for her encouragement.

"I knew she could do it!" she said. "When I saw her out there trying so hard, I just couldn't let her give up. Not when she was so close to making it. That's what I'm here for."

Overcoming the Final Illusion

Perhaps the most difficult part of Deirdre's rehabilitation was the psychological testing which she had to endure. Certain members of the medical team were convinced that she simply *had* to exhibit some degree of brain damage and memory loss. Previous experience taught them that the severe level of edema and subsequent lack of oxygen she experienced *had* to result in brain dysfunction. It was difficult for them to accept that, in this instance, the axiom might not hold true.

The psychological testing was arduous and lengthy. Sometimes a single testing session would last for three hours. Following a short break, the testing would begin again. The battery of tests consisted of hand-eye coordination exercises, memory tests, mental associations, mathematical equations, abstract reasoning, and general intelligence tests, to name a few. In short, Deirdre was bombarded with everything and anything having to do with testing cognitive abilities. She was still in the process of regaining her physical strength, and this grueling schedule proved to be very demanding. At times she was tired, at times she was bored, and at other times she was just fed up with sitting through hours of questions. These factors often accounted for her short attention span. We explained the importance of these procedures to her, but that didn't make it any easier.

Early in the testing, the neuropsychologist in charge was complaining that the test results were not falling within the projected parameters. The results were falling within *normal* parameters, and the doctor was worried that she was missing something. The results couldn't be correct. She said that, given the course of the disease, it was impossible for

Deirdre to have escaped some degree of brain damage. Frustrated, she announced that Deirdre was just not performing according to expectations.

At this point, a young intern assigned to pediatrics responded with a frustration of his own.

"Doctor," he responded, "this case hasn't followed the expected prognosis since it began. Nothing about Deirdre's recovery has ever occurred according to 'expectations.' What makes you think that she would now?"

The intern was trying to point out that this case was setting new, often startling precedents and could not be judged by previous ideas as to the expected course of response.

A good example of Deirdre's typical reaction to the testing came from an incident during a memory exercise. The doctor had just read a passage upon which Deirdre was to base her answers to certain questions. When the doctor asked her, "Where is it cold?" Deirdre, tired and irritable after a long day of questioning, responded with "*Antarctica!*"

Darcie was there at the time, and she said it was all she could do to keep from bursting with laughter. Deirdre was correct. It *was* cold in Antarctica. Unfortunately, this was not the response the doctor was looking for and she didn't hide her exasperation.

"But it *is* cold in Antarctica," Darcie countered. "Doesn't that show that she not only remembers the continent, but also remembers that it has a cold climate? Doesn't it show good memory recall?"

The doctor didn't answer and proceeded with the rest of her questions.

Finally, after a week of lengthy sessions, the neuropsychologists concluded their testing. The final results showed that while Deirdre was still weak in hand-eye coordination and dexterity, conditions expected to improve with time, all other tests were within normal limits. There was no evidence of short- or long-term memory loss and no evidence of any other brain dysfunction. Deirdre had recovered with complete use of all her mental faculties. While we were not in the least bit surprised, it was just another one of the many "unexplainable" facts which baffled the doctors.

Nearing the Top

We were nearing the summit of our long journey and found that, for the first time in many days, we had time to pause and catch our breath. We were high above the clouds now, the sun was shining overhead, and the wind was at our back. Beneath our feet, as far as the eye could see, was the green of new growth that spring brings. As we took a moment to reflect, an awareness of the magnitude of our situation began to dawn, and we slowly started to fathom the enormity of our experience. Our journey had taken us through the valleys of fear and doubt to the very gate of death itself, and through faith, hope, and love led us to the amazing miracle of life. There were only a few steps more to go to reach the pinnacle of the mountain's summit, and we eagerly leapt forward to complete them.

✻ ✻ ✻

To witness a so-called miracle is to stand aside and let God work through you. In any healing work we cultivate the practice of God's presence until it literally takes over. God uses us to express His power and authority to heal. In any healing work, we turn ourself over to God so that His power can pour through us, so that His perfect work can be done through us.

—May Rowland, *The Magic of the Word*

9

Homecoming

Come to the edge, he said.
They said: We are afraid.
Come to the edge, he said.
They came. He pushed them ... and they flew.
—Guillaume Apollinaire

Explorations

A part of Deirdre's therapy involved daily visits to various sections of the hospital via a wheelchair. This allowed her to interact with people and become acclimated to a more normal level of activity. To make it interesting, we made a game of it called "Let's Go Exploring." We never knew what we would find or what "adventures" we might encounter.

One particularly memorable ride occurred when Sharon and Dot were taking Deirdre to the "Sunflower Shop," a store for hospital patients. As they were going down a between-buildings corridor, Sharon paused to admire some flowers and let go of the wheelchair. The corridor was slanted at an angle, and the wheelchair immediately started to roll and gather speed. In an instant, Deirdre found herself fast approaching the far wall and hollered out, *"Aaargh! I'm gonna' get you, Sharon! Aaahhh!"*

Dot was the first to realize what had happened and shouted, *"Quick, grab her!"* as both she and Sharon ran after the wheelchair. Neither got to it in time, however, and it hit the wall. Fortunately, Deirdre had the sense to try to cushion the impact with her feet, and she wasn't any the worse for wear, although Sharon and Dot had an awful fright. Overall, I think Deirdre enjoyed that escapade because it was a story she loved to tell again and again.

In fact, other than the blood draws, Deirdre seemed to be enjoying her final days in the hospital. The diet of clear liquids and Ensure® had given way to solid food, and we sometimes supplemented the usual hospital fare with small samples of her favorites, such as pizza. She also learned that people seemed willing to give her whatever she wanted. One day, seeing Sharon wearing a pink blouse with red roses (her favorite flower) printed on it, she meekly said, in her by now almost comic monotone, "Gee, Sharon. I like that shirt. Wish I had one like it."

When Sharon responded, "You like it? You've got it. It's yours!" the delight on Deirdre's face was evident. It was also evident to me that she was regaining her old sense of self.

Seeing Is Believing. One exploration trip took Deirdre and I to the pediatric ICU where we planned to say hello to some of the nurses. I parked the wheelchair outside, and we walked in. Sitting at the desk, his back to us, was Dr. Chaves, busily doing paperwork. He had fairly well removed himself from Deirdre's case following her transfer to pediatrics and turned it over to Dr. Pardo. As a result, we hadn't had much contact with him in recent days. I remembered his comment about not believing until he saw her "walking and talking" and thought that this must be our opportunity to show him the extent of her recovery. I also wanted him to know that we didn't harbor any ill feelings toward him for not believing she could recover. We knew he had done everything it was in his power to do. He just wasn't prepared for a miracle.

"Dr. Chaves," I called.

He turned around and, upon seeing us, said hello.

"Doctor," I continued, "you said you wanted to see Deirdre when she was walking and talking, and here she is."

"Yes," he said smiling. "You know," he said slowly as if searching for the right words, "I did not believe it was possible. When I left . . . I did not see how she could . . . live beyond the night."

"I know," I said. "None of us knew what would happen. We just had to keep believing in a miracle. But I want to thank you for all you did. We know you did everything possible. But we need to remember what you told us once, that things like this are in God's hands, not ours."

He nodded his head and asked, "Do you know," looking at Deirdre, "you are called 'The Miracle Kid'? You are a very lucky little girl."

Deirdre answered, "Yes," and I could see that she was already tiring so I told Dr. Chaves that we needed to be going. We said good-by and left. I felt that we had made our peace with the doctor.

PREPARATIONS

By the end of Deirdre's first week in pediatrics, Dr. Pardo was considering an early discharge. The medical tests indicated that her physical condition was returning to normal, and the psychological tests had concluded with favorable results. The respiratory therapist stated that her lung condition had improved to the point that it could be treated by breathing exercises at home. The physical therapist reached a similar conclusion, stating that Deirdre could continue her range of motion and dexterity exercises outside of a hospital setting. And although the problem of Deirdre's "lazy eye" and resultant double vision persisted, the prognosis was that the brain edema had pinched a nerve and stretched muscles, a condition which would resolve itself over time. Dr. Pardo was going to wait the weekend and make a decision the following Monday.

Bittersweet Farewells. We spent this weekend in a leisurely manner and began to tie up loose ends in anticipation of saying good-by. Early Saturday, we went to bid Matthew and Janet farewell, as Matthew was being discharged. He had been transferred to pediatrics shortly after Deirdre, but was the first to go home. We had talked to Janet during the week, but this time our talk would end in good-by. That last day we saw him, Matthew seemed very much like a normal, healthy five-year-old boy. As we said farewell, we knew it was likely that this would be the last time we would see this child who had been a fellow traveler on our journey. We wished him continued health and happiness. I know that from time to time, many of us still remember Matthew in prayer.

Throughout the week we had returned to the ICU to visit baby Morgan and her parents. This weekend, however, we were able to visit them in pediatrics, as Morgan had been transferred out of ICU. We shared in their happiness as they told us that the doctors thought Morgan might be well enough to go home by the end of the week. We, in turn, told them that Deirdre would be discharged shortly, and although we would be leaving, we would continue to pray for Morgan's complete recovery. We would not forget the small baby who also had become a part of our journey.

AWAITING DISCHARGE

Last-Minute Distractions. Monday morning did not begin on a good note. After being told Saturday that no more blood samples would be required, a nurse showed up at 5:30 a.m. to make one more draw. Deirdre was frantic and grabbed the television's remote control, swung it back and forth, and told the nurse she would hit her if she came any closer. I was awakened by her cries.

"No more blood!" she cried. "They promised me. No more blood! Mommy, it's the vampire! Please, don't let her take my blood. They told me no more blood!"

I pointed out that we *had* been told that the blood draws were over, and, as this was a new nurse, I showed her the tender scar tissue that already covered both of Deirdre's arms.

"She's had so many needles stuck in her that there's no fresh veins or skin. The last few times the nurse had to find a vein between her fingers and stick her there. Do you really need another sample?"

The nurse replied that she was just following orders. She didn't know what the other nurse had said, but a blood draw was standard procedure prior to discharge. I tried to calm Deirdre and tell her that if she wanted to go home, she had to submit to yet another needle. Through tears and whimpers, I held her while the nurse struggled to find a fresh vein. I couldn't watch. I would be so glad when we could go home.

It wasn't long before Dr. Chaves appeared, along with another doctor I hadn't seen before. They requested permission to perform a liver biopsy. It was the only way to be absolutely certain that Deirdre had Reye's syndrome and not a pseudo-Reye's disease. At this point, however, neither Tino nor I cared about "absolute certainty," and I was upset that they hadn't discussed this procedure earlier. Deirdre was expecting to go home, and now they wanted her to undergo yet another procedure? Our first response was that she had been through enough, and we did not want to subject her to anything more. But we told Dr. Chaves that we would think about it and let him know our decision.

Final Decision. When Dr. Pardo made her daily rounds, we asked her about the biopsy. In her opinion, a biopsy was not really necessary. While it would be helpful for research purposes, it did not impact Deirdre's treatment. Deirdre's case had generated a lot of interest, she told us, because they couldn't explain her recovery. Researchers were very interested in any information about her physical status; the biopsy would be one more bit of data for them to analyze. Hearing this reinforced our original inclination, and Tino and I refused to grant permission for the biopsy.

Then we turned our attention to a more important matter and asked Dr. Pardo about Deirdre's discharge. When she replied, "How about today?" we thought we had heard wrong. We had hoped for discharge tomorrow at the earliest, and now Dr. Pardo was saying today! We couldn't believe it.

All that had to be done, Dr. Pardo said, was to get each therapist and the attending pediatric doctor, Dr. Stein, to complete the final paperwork and prepare discharge instructions. The neuropsychologists would also have to give us a final briefing. She seemed certain that it could be done before the day was over, and we could be on our way by late afternoon.

Before leaving, Dr. Pardo held Deirdre's hand and spoke to her.

"So, now you're well enough to go home," she said. "I just want to tell you what a very special little girl you are. You should have died, you know. And yet you lived. God must have a very special purpose for you, to have brought you back. Never forget that."

HOMEWARD BOUND

With so little time to prepare, there were many things to do. First, there were phone calls, particularly to Dot and Sharon to let them know we were leaving. Then we had to pack up the plants, flowers, gifts, cards, and toys. We also packed certain items which could not be returned, such as slippers, toothbrushes, combs, and the water pitcher. While Darcie and I sat with Deirdre, Tino and Brenda loaded the car as full as they could. Then Darcie and I took the remaining items to my car. Although we had already taken some things home, there was barely room enough for everything between the two vehicles! Deirdre got dressed in the clothes we had brought for this occasion and then we waited.

It wasn't long before everyone had completed his or her part of the paperwork. The physical and respiratory therapists were the first to see us with discharge instructions. Then the neuropsychologists gave us a final brief of their findings. A short time later, Dr. Stein consulted with us, reviewing all findings, the recovery prognosis, and recommendations for follow-up treatment. All we needed was for the administrative officer to sign the final discharge. The papers had been sent hours before, but had not been returned. By mid-afternoon, Tino and Brenda decided to go home and prepare for Deirdre. Darcie and I stayed with Deirdre awaiting the discharge papers.

Hours later we were still waiting, and I, in my usual manner, voiced my concern. Eventually, the head nurse called and presented the final papers for signature. After a quick signature, I received my copy and we were on our way. A nurse accompanied us as we put Deirdre in a wheelchair one last time and took her down to the front entrance. On Monday, March 11, shortly after 5:00 p.m., "The Miracle Kid" walked out of the hospital well on her way to a complete recovery.

Returning Home

After nearly three weeks of inattention, Tino had given our house a quick but thorough cleaning. He set out the plants, flowers, and toys he brought and made sure that everything was in place for Deirdre's arrival.

The car ride was fatiguing for Deirdre, and I realized that it was the first time she had been outside since her hospitalization three weeks ago. She said that everything seemed to "whiz around" her as we drove. Once home, we helped her up the front stairs to the living room, where she promptly collapsed on the couch. Sharon and Dot arrived a short time later, bringing dinner with them. Bill was recovering from his bout of flu and thought it best not to expose Deirdre to any unnecessary contagion. We spent the next few hours in quiet, but happy conversation. Our long journey was over; our arduous struggle had come to an end. We were home now, and things would return to normal. Or so we thought.

The Big Letdown

The first night home passed without incident, and we greeted the morning with thanks for the coming day. For some reason, however, Tino and I felt more melancholic than happy. It was almost as if we were depressed! Even Brenda's early morning arrival didn't do much to raise our spirits, and it wasn't long before we realized that Brenda had similar feelings. More surprisingly, even Deirdre shared this unexplainable reaction. Could we really feel "letdown" at being home?

After some discussion, the answer seemed to be yes. As we talked, we realized that, while in the hospital, we had become accustomed to a high level of continuous concern and activity that a hospital setting generates. We hadn't really had a moment's pause the whole time we were there, and we had grown accustomed to this intense degree of interaction. Once home, that high level of activity had suddenly dropped, and for the first time in weeks we felt very alone. As for Deirdre, she had been the center of attention for a long time; she had even come to enjoy her last few days in the hospital. But now the layers of people who had surrounded her were gone. We realized that it would take time for all of us to adjust to a more normal level of activity.

Brenda further pointed out that it was quite likely our energy levels had dropped because the number of people praying for us had decreased once they learned Deirdre was out of the hospital. It was possible that a good number of people equated discharge with wellness and no longer saw a need for prayer. As a result, the prayer energy which had been directed toward us had dropped as well, and we were not receiving the support we had come to count on.

It was necessary, Brenda said, to let people know that "they have to keep praying, possibly for a long time." She immediately called Silent Unity and the A.R.E. Glad Helpers and requested that they continue their prayers for the next thirty days. Then she called Mary and asked her to contact members within our Unity church to ensure that they continued their prayers also. Finally, we called our families and friends and explained that, although Deirdre was home, we still needed their prayers as much as ever.

WHEN PAIN AND FEAR PERSIST

Tuesday afternoon, Deirdre was taking a nap when she suddenly cried out in pain.

"Mommy, it hurts," she said. "My head hurts so much. Make it go away!"

Tino, Brenda, and I rushed upstairs to find her holding her head, rocking in pain. She had never complained of head pain while in the hospital, and our first thought was that somehow the brain edema had returned. She continued to cry out loud while we tried to determine what the problem was. I immediately put in a call to Dr. Pardo, but she was on rounds and unavailable. The nurse assured me that she would return my call. In the interim, she recommended that I give Deirdre Tylenol® for the pain.

Deirdre took the Tylenol®, and I suggested she try to sleep so that it could work better. "No, I can't go to sleep," she yelled. "The last time I went to sleep when I hurt, I woke up in the hospital. The same thing will happen again. I don't want to go into a coma again. I won't go to sleep! *I won't go to sleep ever again!*" she repeated adamantly.

This outburst made me realize that Deirdre still had a deep-seated fear that her sickness would come back. She was not only in physical pain, but she felt emotional pain as well. She was terrified of closing her eyes and going to sleep. She insisted that I lay next to her and hold her head and her hand.

"Make it stop hurting, Mommy," she begged again.

Lying next to her, I put my left hand on her head and held her right hand with mine. I told her to imagine that the pain was being drawn out of her head and passing into my hand and up my arm where it disappeared. I told her that with my right hand, I was sending healing energy into her body and to picture it spreading to the places where it hurt. I talked to her quietly, outlining this flow of energy over and over.

As I held Deirdre, I realized that we had learned a great deal in the past three weeks. The initial fear I felt when she first cried out in pain had quickly disappeared, replaced by the belief that we possessed within us the ability to deal with this situation. I felt comfortable working with energy now and allowed myself to be guided by my inner voice. Somehow, I intuitively knew that the pain was part of Deirdre's recovery process, almost as if her own body's energies were fluctuating as they returned to a normal balance and flow. I also knew that Deirdre and I could work through this together. I continued to talk to her, emphasizing that the pain was becoming less and less. I encouraged her to fall asleep, reassuring her that she was safe now and nothing could happen to her. She resisted at first, but exhaustion finally won out and she drifted off to sleep. I stayed with her a while longer. When she awoke a few hours later, the pain was gone.

Dr. Pardo did return my call some hours later. She explained that Deirdre had received so many drugs during her illness that it was only natural for her to experience some pain and discomfort as her body readjusted. Headaches and other pain were not uncommon, she said, and could continue for a while. As long as the Tylenol® worked, there was no need to worry. The only symptom we had to be concerned about, however, was vomiting. If Deirdre ever became nauseous and began to vomit, we were to bring her to the hospital immediately.

While Dr. Pardo's assessment eased our fears, we also realized that Deirdre's recovery was going to involve more than we had expected. Things were not automatically going to become "all right" just because we had come home. Indeed, for the next two weeks, Deirdre suffered at least one unbearable headache each day. Each time I repeated the same procedure. Recovery was going to take time, patience, and effort.

MARK OF A SHAMAN

A few days later, Deirdre cried out as she always did when a headache began. This time, however, she was shouting for a different reason—she was shouting about her hair.

"It's gone. My hair is gone. What happened to my hair?"

When she calmed down, she told me that while combing her hair, she found a huge bald spot at the back of her head. It scared her. As I lifted her hair out of the way, I did see a bald spot totally devoid of hair. What was most peculiar, however, was the fact that this bald spot formed a perfectly symmetrical circle two inches in diameter. It looked as if someone had literally shaved this area, but we knew this was impossible. It also seemed strange that we had not noticed it before. Brenda hadn't seen it when she first combed out Deirdre's hair, nor did we notice any hair strands on combs or pillows. We were at a loss to explain it until Tino spoke up. He had heard of this before in Native American folklore. Among certain tribes, including his own, it was considered the sign of a shaman.

After hearing this explanation, we shared it with Deirdre, and she seemed satisfied. Her main concern was that she would lose more hair, but once we assured her that wouldn't happen, she seemed content, and we took no further action. Her hair was long enough to cover that spot so that it couldn't be seen except upon close examination.

Some time later, our hairdresser Trisha told us that this is a recognized medical condition called *alopecia,* which sometimes occurs during disease or following severe trauma. While its exact cause is unknown, it has been attributed to certain drugs or to stress. Other cultures have a different explanation, however, and believe it is used to "mark" a person who has been chosen to walk in both the physical world and the spirit world. It normally appears following completion of that person's quest or vision. It is, as Tino told us, the mark of a shaman.

CIRCLE OF LOVE

The problems we encountered those first few days at home prompted Brenda to recommend that we continue a practice we had begun in the hospital. Oftentimes we had gathered together in the consultation room, forming a circle and holding hands while we joined in prayer. Now Brenda suggested that we take this a step further and add another element, namely, raising energy and directing that energy to where it was needed.

We came together as we had so often, bonding in love and prayer. After grounding ourselves and saying a prayer of protection, someone would begin with a verbal prayer, and we would go around the circle, adding to the prayer as we wanted. Then we would spend a few minutes in meditation. When we were finished, the person who led the prayer would speak again and take the energy/love/light, visualize it growing in strength and intensity, move it around the circle, and send it in and through us, eventually directing it to the person or condition needing prayer.

We did this each time we met, even if it there were only three or four of us. Sometimes we included Deirdre and Sara in our circle, and one time we asked Mary to join us. If someone was particularly in need, we had the person stand in the middle of the circle and focused the energy toward him or her. We found that this form of prayer had the effect of energizing us and helped us keep our physical and mental strength high.

On the Road to Health

We had been advised to allow Deirdre at least two weeks of rest at home before having her return to school. This seemed appropriate and, considering that her second week at home coincided with spring break, it meant one less week of missed classes. While at home, she continued to practice her physical therapy and breathing exercises. She also had plenty of practice walking because our house consists of four levels, and she had to use the stairs to go from one area to another. Although she still had double vision, she was learning to adapt to it and slowly became accustomed to seeing in duplicate.

Working with Deirdre's rehabilitation required a great deal of time and effort. I was fortunate to have sixty days of leave on the books and was able to take as much time as I needed. Tino had been granted a leave of absence, although that meant a loss of his salary for several weeks. We were fortunate to have Darcie stay with us and help for another two weeks.

As we continued to work toward Deirdre's recovery, however, we realized the importance of returning to a more normal routine. Darcie made plans to return to Boston, and Tino and I decided that it would soon be time for us to return to work. Tino would return following her first week at home, while I would stay home another week until she began school. Since Tino worked the night shift, one of us was always home with Deirdre.

Birthday Celebration

Resuming a normal routine also meant taking Deirdre out in public and trying to acclimate her back into daily activities. At first she showed some reluctance at being seen in public, due to her drooping eye and the still-mending scar on her forehead. There was one occasion, however, for which she needed no encouragement—her eleventh birthday celebration. Deirdre turned eleven on March 20, and we honored her request to have a dinner party at a local restaurant. Sharon, Brenda, Brad, Sara, Dot, Bill, and Darcie joined us. As she blew out the candles on her birthday cake, I thought of how close we had come to not seeing this day. Had it not been for God's loving miracle, this would have been a very different day indeed.

School Days

Upon Deirdre's release from the hospital, I picked up homework assignments so that she could begin to catch up on her school work. We had expected that once Deirdre returned to school, she would do so full time. It soon became apparent, however, that she still tired easily and required a nap each afternoon. After speaking with Mrs. Kramer, the school nurse, and her teachers, we decided that it would be best if Deirdre returned on a half-day basis.

The day she returned, she was greeted by a banner signed by the staff, teachers, and many, many students. Mrs. Witte had arranged for a cake and the class held a party in her honor. She also assured Deirdre that she had taken care of all the paperwork necessary to enter her science project in the Research & Development (R&D) Forum. When Deirdre returned home after her first day, I could see that she was overwhelmed by this show of affection.

The teachers were very accommodating about tailoring homework assignments and giving her additional attention to help her make up for lost ground. They also gave her more verbal than written work to ease the strain on her vision. In fact, the entire staff was willing to do everything possible to ensure that Deirdre had no trouble catching up with her classmates. I will always be grateful for their concern and understanding.

COMING FULL CIRCLE

As the weeks passed, Deirdre slowly regained her strength and our lives began to return to normal. By late April, she began attending school full time and even started to participate in gym class on a limited basis. The day of the R&D Forum arrived, and Deirdre's science project took a first-place blue ribbon. She was ecstatic! All that hard work had paid off. When she returned to Unity Church for the first time, the Sunday school celebrated with a "welcome back" party complete with cake. It wasn't long before she was taking care of the nursery children once again.

Easter Message. Easter was particularly poignant for us that year. Sharon, Brenda, Brad, and Sara joined us for church services. When the Sunday school sang, I saw Mary looking over at Deirdre with tears in her eyes. I knew they were the same tears of joy we all shared. I also knew that we were sharing the same thought. We couldn't help but compare our miracle with another miracle that occurred that first Easter Sunday.

Jesus Christ has taught us that we are more than these bodies we inhabit; we are spiritual beings, sons and daughters of the Creator God, heirs to His good kingdom. Through His death and resurrection, Jesus demonstrated this truth for all humankind and beyond. By assuming the cross, He showed that even though the body be killed, you do not die. He chose the most torturous death to offer us proof that although the body be scourged, scarred, and mutilated, the soul cannot be harmed and remains forever eternal. As the Christ soul was able to overcome physical law to heal and reanimate His broken body, so, too, was Deirdre's diseased body healed. We had witnessed firsthand the fulfillment of the promise and hope of that first Easter Sunday.

Walk to Health.   In April, Deirdre's school announced that it would be participating in a five kilometer walk/run to be held on Mother's Day. It was sponsored by the Rotary to benefit local charities. Her school would be competing with two other schools for prizes. Much to my surprise, Deirdre announced that she intended to participate! I had long tried, without success, to interest her in walking or jogging. Now, not more than a month out of the hospital, she showed an interest in attempting this race. I thought about it and realized that it might actually be good therapy, so I agreed to help her with a paced regimen of training.

When Sharon heard that we were going to participate, she decided to participate as well, and the three of us showed up at the 6:30 a.m. check-in on race day. It was an ideal morning for a race, not too hot and not too cold, with only a mild breeze. In practice, Deirdre had walked up to three miles, although it had been at a much slower pace. As we passed the two-mile mark, she indicated that she was tiring. There was no turning back, however, and we pressed on. After another half mile she said, "I don't know if I can make it. I feel like I'm going to die."

Sharon and I looked at each other and began to laugh.

"You already tried that once," we told her, "and it didn't work. You'll just have to finish the race."

We received an exasperated look in return, but not too long after that she regained her second wind and triumphantly crossed the finish line with a time of 48 minutes, 12 seconds. After the last walkers had finished, all the participants gathered for the presentation of prizes. We were pleased to hear that Deirdre's school had won the school competition, and all the children were asked to stay for pictures. That picture serves as a constant reminder of this unbelievable accomplishment for a child who only two months earlier lay comatose at death's door. It was just another example of the marvelous power that mind and spirit can exert over the human body.

School's Out. By the time the school year came to a close, Deirdre had made up all of the work she had missed. With her teacher's help and encouragement and a lot of hard work, she was able to complete the fifth grade with the rest of her class and be promoted to the sixth grade.

Three-Month Checkup. Shortly after school was dismissed for the summer, Deirdre returned to UKMC for her three-month checkup. At first she was wary of returning to the hospital, but I tried to turn it into a fun outing with the promise of a trip to the gift shop and lunch at the cafeteria which she liked so much. This was one of the few hospitals that actually served good food.

The appointment was scheduled with Dr. Pardo, and as soon as she entered the examination room, she greeted Deirdre with, "Hello there, 'Miracle Girl.' How have you been?"

As she proceeded with a thorough physical examination, she asked extensive questions about Deirdre's progress and activities during the last three months. When she concluded her examination, she told us that Deirdre had exceeded all expectations and that they couldn't have charted a better recovery. Although the double vision persisted, Deirdre's eye had shown a great deal of improvement, and there was every reason to believe that this would continue. She recommended that we continue our appointments at the eye clinic. Other than that, Deirdre had a clean bill of health.

Then Dr. Pardo echoed the sentiment she had expressed once before and told Deirdre that she hoped she realized just how special she was and how close to death she had come. She repeated that God must have a special purpose for her and that was why she lived.

As the appointment came to a close, Dr. Pardo said we would not have to return until March of next year, for a one-year checkup. Before we left, I asked her if it would be possible to see Dr. Chaves. She went to find him and a short time later he appeared. After greeting us, he told us that Dr. Pardo had briefed him on Deirdre's excellent recovery. As we talked, he told us again that the night he had left the ICU, he did not believe she would be alive when he returned.

"In fact," he said, "there were *two* children in there who I thought would be gone (dead) when I returned. I had not expected to see them again."

I knew that he meant Deirdre and Matthew. I told him that a Higher Power had been at work. We agreed that God had worked more than one miracle that week.

"I know," he replied. "As I told you once, these things are in God's hands." And then looking at Deirdre, he said, "You are a very lucky girl. Dr. Pardo thinks God has a special purpose planned for you. She may be right."

Then we said good-by and headed for the gift shop.

Summer Fun. Deirdre spent most of the summer at the swimming pool with her friend Jenny. We also had a visit from my mother Esther and one from my aunt Ida. In July we took an extended trip to Colorado, New Mexico, and Arizona and paid a visit to Tino's family. Each family reunion was marked by hugs and tears of joy.

A Gift of Spirit.   Perhaps the most momentous occasion of that summer involved the fulfillment of a hospital promise. Deirdre had wanted a dog for years, but circumstances were such that it had not been possible. While in the hospital, Tino and I promised Deirdre that if she got well, we would find a way to get her a dog. In June, we were able to fulfill that promise.

A fellow service member had started to breed the type of dog that had long been Deirdre's favorite—miniature dachshunds. Knowing of our promise, he offered us one of the pups from the first litter. The pups were only five days old when we took Deirdre to see them. The visit was a surprise, and when she saw those four tiny pups and realized she could have her pick, it was the first and only time that I have seen her speechless. She chose a female, the runt of the litter, and held her in the palm of her hand. Then Tino held her and announced that her name was "Spirit." The pup turned her head, opened one eye, and looked straight at him. We knew he was right.

Spirit is a member of our family now and with her "high-spirited" nature certainly lives up to her name. She has brought us much humor, joy, and love, and we thank the Almighty Spirit that she has come to share our life.

Return to School.   As summer drew to a close, we turned our thoughts to the start of the new school year. Deirdre's double vision was nearly corrected now, and by October it would be completely resolved. Other than a faint small scar on her forehead, there was nothing to indicate the trauma she had endured.

Final Checkup.   In March 1992, Deirdre returned to UKMC for a one-year checkup. After giving her a clean bill of health, Dr. Chaves told us that in the year following her admission, they had treated two other cases of Reye's syndrome, both with successful results. Then he told us that she had been the first patient to recover from Reye's in over two years, and he felt that it marked a turning point of some sort. He further told us that one of the boys treated after her had sunk into a coma nearly as deep as hers. And although he would not have previously thought recovery was possible, he thought back to Deirdre and knew that, if she had lived, this boy could live also.

Then Dr. Chaves made an unusual request. He asked to take Deirdre's picture for use in their lectures on Reye's syndrome. The case had become part of the medical school's curriculum on this disease, and he and Dr. Pardo felt that a visual picture had a stronger impact on the students. It made the case more personal, he said. Deirdre, of course, happily complied.

On Reaching the Summit

At long last, we had come to the end of our upward journey. We had reached the mountain summit. As we looked out upon the scenery below us, we realized that our eyes were seeing things in new and unique ways. Each color had a vibrancy and radiance which had hitherto gone unnoticed, and the rays of the sun shone with a brightness we had never perceived. The smells of the earth and the feel of the wind registered with new, intense feelings. The sun was directly overhead and all trace of shadow had vanished.

It was as if we were seeing the true beauty of the world for the first time. And indeed we were, for a consequence of reaching the summit is a change in perception. Once you reach the mountain's pinnacle, you will never look on the world in the same way again, for you now understand its true reality. The fogged illusion of fear and doubt have lifted, and you see only through the eyes of love.

Although our path had ended and we had reached our long-sought goal, we would soon learn that our journey was not yet over. In fact, in some ways it had only just begun, for the learning would continue for a long time to come. With Deirdre now completely recovered, it was time to pause and reflect upon the journey we had made and consider the new world which lay before us.

✴ ✴ ✴

The real voyage of discovery consists not in seeking new lands, but in seeing with new eyes. —Marcel Proust

10

Reflections from the Mountaintop

Come, let us go up to the mountain of the Lord. He will teach us His ways so that we may walk in His paths.
                                                        —Micah 4:2

The Mountain Summit

OUR journey was now nearing its end. We had gone from the depths of despair to the heights of joy. With the rigors of this arduous trek behind us, we found ourselves standing on the brink of new heights we had never before thought possible. We had reached the mountain's summit and come face to face with its miracle peak. Upon reaching this pinnacle, we found that we were able to see with a new, clear vision we had not previously possessed. It was time for all of us to pause and reflect upon our journey in spirit.

RETROSPECTIVE VISION: CLUES WE MISSED

One of the most puzzling aspects of our journey was that no one seemed to know ahead of time that we were about to face one of the most momentous experiences of our lives. Many of us had been accustomed to receiving information through meditation and dreams, yet not one of us was aware that we had received warning signs of Deirdre's approaching crisis. With the wisdom of reflective hindsight, however, we realized that we had indeed been given information regarding Deirdre's coming ordeal. We had just misinterpreted the clues and failed to understand their meaning.

Precognitive Dreams. Approximately three months prior to Deirdre's illness Bill had a dream in which he asked me if Deirdre had ever been hospitalized. In the dream I responded no, saying that she had always been very healthy. Then I paused, adding that I had almost forgotten about the one time she had been hospitalized and had a hole drilled into her head. Since everything had turned out all right in the dream, I didn't think much about it any more.

This dream puzzled Bill and during study group one evening, he recounted it. We discussed it briefly, but we couldn't come up with a viable interpretation. While we thought it unusual, we never discussed the dream any further and promptly forgot it. Even during Deirdre's hospitalization, no one recalled the dream. It wasn't until some weeks after her release from the hospital that Bill remembered it again. We knew by then that it *had* been a precognitive dream. It was just that we had not realized it at the time.

The World Exploded. Around the same time as Bill's dream, Deirdre also had a dream which warned of the impending crisis. Once again, however, we misinterpreted the information we were given.

Deirdre was usually reluctant to discuss her dreams, and on the few occasions she did, I knew that they held some special significance. The dream she told us concerned a time when the world was in danger of exploding. In the dream, she was with a group of scientists and doctors who wore white lab coats. All the people and their families had been evacuated to another planet and were safe. Deirdre and the scientists were working to save the world and prevent it from exploding. Despite their efforts, however, they were unable to stop the impending destruction. Knowing there was nothing left to do, they boarded the last spaceship and escaped from earth prior to the explosion. Although she saw the world explode through the ship's portal, she knew that everything would be all right, because we (her family) and all the other people were safe and would soon be reunited on a new world.

At the time she told us this dream, we thought of two possible interpretations. One possibility was that the dream referred to probable changes in her life, changes which would seem to destroy her old world, but were really part of the normal growth process we all encounter during the adolescent years. Another possibility was that the dream referred to what many believe to be upcoming earth changes. While the world as we know it would "pass away," the people would survive and find a new life in a new world.

Once again, we had missed the true meaning of the dream, a dream no one recalled until weeks after Deirdre's recovery. It was clear then that this dream had foretold of her illness. The team of scientists working to save the world represented the medical team who fought so valiantly to save her life. The fact that they failed indicated that we would have to rely on means other than medical science. Just as the world exploded in the dream, Deirdre's world exploded, for it would never again be the same after her illness. As in the dream, however, she herself was safe, and she and the others started a new life by going to the stars.

This journey to the stars represented a raising of consciousness and showed that this experience would have a transformative effect; in essence, change our perception of the world we knew.

Shamanic Vision. There was one other occurrence which preceded Deirdre's illness, and although it did not foretell of the upcoming crisis, we later realized that its appearance and timing played an important role in the drama which was about to unfold.

Three months prior to Deirdre's illness, Tino, Deirdre, and I took a vacation to New Mexico, accompanied by Brenda, her daughter Sara, and Sharon. They had never been to the Southwest and we wanted to show them this wonderful part of the country. We also planned on visiting several "sacred sites" and regarded the trip as more of an insightful adventure than a pleasure trip.

One of our stops included the Anasazi ruins at Aztec, New Mexico. While pausing to meditate in the reconstructed Great Kiva of Aztec, Deirdre had what can only be described as a psychic experience. She sat with Sharon near the fire pit in the center of the kiva. Tino and I sat on one side of the kiva, while Brenda and Sara sat on the other. The four of us knew that something odd had happened, for as soon as Sharon closed her eyes to meditate, we felt a strong gust of wind blow down into the kiva. For the next few moments, everything became eerily quiet. I saw Deirdre staring motionlessly ahead, her eyes wide open. After a few minutes she closed them tight, lowered her head, and squeezed Sharon's hand.

A short time later Sharon finished her meditation. She seemed unaware that anything unusual had happened. Deirdre, however, was quick to leave the kiva and remained unusually quiet for the rest of the day.

She was reluctant to discuss what had happened and we respected her privacy. However, when she opened up a few days later and described her experience, we knew that she had what can only be described as a "vision" in the Native American tradition. According to tradition, a vision is not normally shared with people other than family or close friends and rarely with those outside the person's tribe. Deirdre has asked me not to reveal its contents to protect her privacy, and I am honoring that request. I can say, however, that the vision was one which gave her a glimpse into the past and for her confirmed the reality of past lives. It also gave her quite a fright, and for a long time she feared the experience would return. We knew that an event like this was of major significance, but we had no way of knowing what it foreshadowed. We know now that it was necessary it occur before Deirdre entered the coma, for it validated and confirmed her belief that life was eternal.

REFLECTIVE VISION: THE JOURNEY UNFOLDS

As we continued to reflect upon our journey, we asked ourselves why we had been led to this path in the first place. Had it been some random quirk of fate which led us here, or was there a method to this madness, a reason we did not understand?

On the Path. The Edgar Cayce readings clearly indicate that "there are no accidents" and that everything happens for a reason. This concept has been called "meaningful coincidence" or "synchronicity." These coincidences are "signals" of a sort from the Universal Mind, designed to guide and direct us. "In each of our lives occur mysterious coincidence—sudden, unexplained events that, once interpreted correctly, serve to guide and direct our actions."[1]

I accept the school of thought which says that each soul, prior to entering the earth plane, is shown each possibility it might have to encounter and, through free will, is given the choice to accept or reject those experiences. During this process, the soul often agrees to accept those situations which will further its spiritual growth or serve as a teaching example for others even though it is aware that the experience may cause hardship on a physical or emotional level. The Cayce readings indicate that it is oftentimes an "advanced" soul who chooses to accept this path to help teach one's fellow brethren. When we enter the earth plane, all knowledge of these possibilities is removed from our conscious memory. The choices we make and the actions we take as we live out our lives determine the course of our path and which possibilities we actually encounter.

Believing this to be true, we had to accept that we had not been placed in this situation by a roll of the dice, by the divine whim of some mysterious being whose motives could not be understood, or by some impersonal decision of the universe. This experience was the culmination of interrelated events being played out during the course of our lives. We had come to this point because of the choices we all had made and actions we had taken and the lessons we still needed to learn.

Precursors.   The first meaningful coincidence we could identify was the sequence of events which had brought our A.R.E. study group together in the first place. We had all originated from different parts of the country, yet for a time we found ourselves drawn together as a group in Kansas City. Add to this the fact that my navy tour there had been unexpectedly extended, and we could clearly see that events were working to bring us together and keep us together so that we could participate in this experience as a group.

Next, was it really mere chance that had led us to the spiritual tools we would use on this journey? Years of familiarity with the concepts in the Cayce readings, Tino's encounter with Unity teachings a few years earlier, our new association with the Unity Church "for Deirdre's sake," Brenda's insistence on attending the "Unity Basics" course, and our recent exposure to the concepts of *A Course in Miracles* were not random happenings, but the result of

Spirit preparing us for the journey ahead.

Further, was it random circumstance that Deirdre had been admitted to a progressive teaching hospital, which was not only a leading center in Reye's syndrome research and treatment, but was tolerant toward nontraditional healing therapies? I have visited other hospitals since our stay at UKMC and realize that many hospitals would not have been as supportive of our efforts as the UKMC staff. My confusion in the emergency room and inability to choose a hospital were a blessing in disguise for they allowed Spirit to make the choice for me. Is it really any surprise that God would ensure that we were in a hospital that provided the most conducive environment possible?

Guideposts on the Path. One of the first meaningful coincidences which drew our attention was the angelic presence reported by many people. People sensed, heard, or even saw angelic beings. Even those who had no prior interest in the paranormal reported such phenomena. Upon regaining consciousness, Deirdre requested the story of a boy carried by an angel, an action that has to be seen as more than random chance. Her quick mention of angels served a twofold purpose. First, it confirmed for her that her memories of being in the presence of angels were real. Second, it validated our belief that we had been surrounded by these holy beings.

Another coincidence involved similarities in the actions of different healers, all of whom, without prompting, seemed to concentrate their healing efforts on the liver and brain stem areas. While the liver and brain are the two areas of the body most severely attacked by the Reye's virus, these people had no way of knowing this for they were not familiar with the diagnosed course of the disease. But while the similarities in their healing efforts reassured us that they were being guided by a Higher Power, we were at a loss to explain why they concentrated on the brain stem rather than the cranium where the edema was localized. Even they could not explain it, but simply felt that for whatever reason this area needed attention.

The importance of the brain stem appeared again during a meditation experience. While meditating on how to best help Deirdre, Sharon was shown the outline of a body in which the brain stem glowed with a blue light. Suddenly, the body lit up, as if it had been electrified, and she clearly saw the "branches" of light spreading through the body. She felt that this meditation meant that she should direct her healing energy to this area, a practice she began to follow.

It would be quite some time before we finally understood the significance of the brain stem in the healer's work on Deirdre. It should be no surprise that it was Sharon who found the missing piece of this puzzle, as months later she discussed our experience with a friend. He told her of an ancient Hindu belief which holds that the brain stem or *medulla oblongata* is the point at which the soul reenters the body following a temporary absence, such as astral travel or a near-death experience. He felt certain that this is why the healers had been unconsciously drawn to this area. Was Sharon's conversation with her friend a coincidence or confirmation to us that the soul does return through a portal at this site, a site which had to be cleared or healed prior to Deirdre's return? Was this perhaps the reason why so many healers directed their healing energies to this particular part of her body?

Omens. Another coincidence discovered in our retrospective discussions connected two seemingly unrelated events separated by the span of four months; namely, Deirdre's vision in the Great Kiva and the *alopecia* or hair loss she experienced after she arrived home. Within Native American tradition, both are considered signs that a person has been "chosen by the spirits." At the time of Deirdre's vision, however, I am not even sure if she was aware of what a "vision" was or what significance it held. Her reaction seemed to indicate that it took her completely by surprise.

It certainly was not something she had consciously sought out. She surely didn't know that a certain kind of *alopecia* was considered to be the mark of a shaman. Yet both of these events occurred in her young life and to us are evidence that synchronicity was at play in revealing these two clues to Deirdre's life mission.

REFLECTIVE VISION: THE PRAYER NETWORK

Of all the aspects of our miracle, perhaps the most astounding was the prayer network itself. As by now may be obvious, the diversity of the prayer network which became involved in Deirdre's healing was unusual to say the least. Within a few days, this network stretched from coast to coast and involved over 650 people. Add to this the known number of churches, sixteen in all, which included Deirdre in their weekly prayers, and you have an additional 1,500 people who were involved in the prayer effort in some way during that first week. Further, a Wiccan periodical, with a circulation of over 1,000, carried a request for prayer on Deirdre's behalf, and we learned later that dozens of readers had responded to that request.

This prayer network spread primarily through word-of-mouth, person-to-person networking. Other than the telephone calls we had made to the A.R.E. Glad Helpers and Silent Unity, people learned of Deirdre's plight through informal means and joined in prayer for no other reason than to help another. Superficial differences in theological orientation were set aside as these people united to help cure a child. The prayer energy they generated was tremendous, and their combined efforts were no doubt a major factor in turning near death into a miraculous recovery. Can you imagine what humans could accomplish if this type of cooperative effort happened on a regular basis?

As I was writing the final chapters of this book, an incident occurred which reminded me once again of the amazing scope of this prayer network. I share it here for it serves as an excellent reminder of the extensive scope of the network. While we know of the groups who participated in the prayer network and are aware of many of the individuals who became involved, it is possible that we will never know of all the people who joined in our prayer effort.

While at a conference in Newport, Rhode Island, I met a fellow naval officer whom I had known casually some years before when he was stationed at a remote reserve center in Missouri. I hadn't had any contact with him in over three years, however. After greeting me, he immediately asked how my daughter was doing. He said he remembered how sick she had been, had prayed for her at the time, and wondered how everything had turned out. Imagine my surprise, for I didn't even know that he knew Deirdre had been ill! Like many others, he found out through word of mouth. When I told him that Deirdre would soon graduate from eighth grade and was looking forward to high school, he smiled and said that it was experiences like these which make you realize what is truly important in life.

INNER VISION: REMEMBRANCES

Reflection on the miracle process would not be complete without consideration of Deirdre's experiences while in an astral or spiritual plane. In fact, the question I am asked most frequently is, "What does she remember?" Given the recent interest in near-death experiences in many circles, this perhaps should not be so surprising. I have the feeling that many people hope that Deirdre remembers something of her experience, so that they can look to it as a validation of their own hopes and beliefs of life beyond death.

It was a long time before Deirdre would discuss her memories. We had asked her some questions, but she seemed reluctant to discuss it, so we did not pursue it further. We realized that it might take time before she was willing to talk about anything she might have remembered. Other than talking about Jesus and the angels, we had never discussed any information with her, partly because we did not want to overwhelm our ten-year-old daughter and partly because we did not want to unduly influence her own recollections. We reassured her that any memories she might have could well be real and that we would be happy to discuss them at a time when she felt comfortable doing so.

Memories. Shortly after coming home from the hospital, Deirdre told us that she remembered hearing a female voice speaking to her in Laguna, the native language of her father's people. She felt sure that this was the voice of her grandmother Jessie, who had passed on two months earlier. When I asked her if she could remember what her grandmother had said, she gave me a funny look and said, "*You know I don't understand Indian.*" I told her that although she might not consciously understand, it was likely that she did understand on a subconscious level and when she needed to know it, the information would be available to her.

Tino and I recalled how Jessie had always spoken to Deirdre in the native tongue. This didn't seem unusual when we lived on the Laguna Pueblo reservation when Deirdre was young, but it continued years later after we had moved away. Yet, while she continued to address Deirdre in Laguna, she often spoke English to her other grandchildren and great grandchildren, who still lived on the reservation and had a greater comprehension of the native language. Deirdre neither spoke nor understood Laguna, yet she always understood her grandmother. We believe that Jessie taught Deirdre during those conversations, but we can only speculate what the lessons might have been.

It would be nearly three years before Deirdre would discuss any other memories. We had long felt that she did remember things, but for whatever reason wasn't willing to share them. Whether the writing of this book served as an impetus or whether the time was just right, I do not know. Whatever the reason, Deirdre suddenly began to share her memories.

She remembered being in four distinct "places": "God's house," although she knew it wasn't a house in the physical sense; a field filled with yellow flowers, where she played with a dog and flew through the air; a beach, where she chased seagulls; and a library, which contained many books. She described seeing an unusual bright light, which radiated out in all directions whenever she "moved" from one "scene" to another. She also described an intense feeling of "belonging," a feeling of total acceptance and a sense of "being home."

She described God's house as having a pinkish-white background, frequented by many angels. It was here that she remembered being with Jesus, and she expressed surprise that I knew He had held her in His lap. She recalled sitting in the middle of a circle, surrounded by many souls or entities. They were engaged in lengthy conversations. Specifically, she saw her grandmother Jessie and also my father Jerry, who had passed away two years before she was born. She also remembered meeting a man whom she at first thought was Tino's father, but later realized that it was Tino's brother who had died many years before she was born. She told of additional entities whom she simply referred to as "the others." When I questioned her as to who they were, she expressed a slight annoyance and repeated, "You know, the others who come when you need help."

She described the library as being a dim grayish color, like stone. She entered a small room with shelves of huge books which stretched up into the sky farther than she could see. There was a pedestal in the room and an old-fashioned lamp. All she had to do was think of the book she wanted, and it moved by itself to the pedestal where she could read it.

After hearing Deirdre describe her memories, I made a comment to the effect that I always knew that she remembered what had happened.

"Of course, I remember," she said. "Why do you think I asked to hear those stories about the footprints and the angel? I needed to know if what I remembered was real."

Then I asked her why she had gone to the library—the akashic records—and her answer was simply, "I wanted to find out what was going to happen when I came back."

When asked why she had gone to the field and the beach, she responded with a typical child's answer that "It was fun." She said that the dog who was playing with her in the field was our dog Spirit, who came to us the summer following Deirdre's recovery.

Deirdre's memories confirmed much of the information we had received about her activities on the astral plane and paralleled much of what we thought had been happening. The activities at God's house substantiated Mary's impression that Deirdre had been involved in a celestial coaching session, the fact that she had been in the Christ presence and the presence of angels. Her memory of the library corroborated our belief that she had gone to the akashic records. Her visits to the field and beach verified that she had gone off to play and had needed to be "called home." It certainly authenticated my impression that she was chasing seagulls on a beach.

Reasons Why. Now that we knew where Deirdre had been, Tino and I asked her if she knew anything about the "why" of this experience. She not only confirmed some of our previous ideas, but provided new insights as well.

Deirdre believes that the main reason for this experience was to serve as a lesson that life is eternal; there is life after death. She said that although many of us *thought* this was true, we did not really *believe* it at the heart level. We needed a demonstration which would prove this truth to us beyond the shadow of a doubt. Prior to her birth, she had been told of the need for this lesson. Although she was not told the details, she was told that there would be a sequence of events that would accomplish this purpose *if* she would agree to it. She already knew the reality of life after death, and so she volunteered to undertake this task to help others know it as well. Deirdre, however, like all souls, retained no conscious memory of the agreements made before birth. It was only after the coma that she became conscious of this memory.

She further said that the healers who came to the hospital to help us were there more as teachers than as students. They knew the truth of eternal life and had come to share their knowledge with us, thereby repaying old debts. She also told us that her illness had not been expected to last as long as it did, but that we were slow to learn the lesson set before us.

Needless to say, this information took some time to digest and contemplate. While we accept Deirdre's insights as correct, we feel they tell only part of the story. While the primary reason behind the miracle may have been to demonstrate that we are spiritual beings whose existence is eternal, it held many other lessons as well, and we still believe that past-life influences played a role in the unfolding of this drama. It is quite possible that it is not yet time for Deirdre to confront the more personal aspects of her experience, although we believe she will address them in time.

Further, we believe that it was necessary for events to unfold as they did in order to afford the time required for certain elements of the miracle to come into play. A quick cure would have left room for speculation that the medical treatment had been responsible for the recovery. It would have altered the size and scope of the prayer network because there would not have been adequate time for it to form and expand. Nor would it have afforded the opportunity necessary for the healers to become involved as they did. The crisis had to build in scope and intensity and reach the threshold of death itself to allow the miracle to manifest as it did. The longer the illness was prolonged, the greater the demonstration that recovery *was* a miracle. It is likely that Deirdre had a different perception of time while in the spiritual plane and that may be why she felt it was "taking too long."

I asked Deirdre why it had taken so long for her to talk about her memories. Why bring it up now? She replied quite simply that perhaps we were now ready to hear it. And with a smile, she added that perhaps she was now ready to tell it.

A NEAR-DEATH EXPERIENCE

Deirdre's recollections closed the loop on defining her experience as a near-death experience (NDE). It met the accepted criteria: heart failure or brain death while in a coma; memories of a Supreme Being, angels, or deceased loved ones; a bright light; an intense feeling of love and peace or, as she described it, a feeling of "belonging"; knowledge of activities on the physical plane; and unexplainable recovery.[2] Like many people who experience an NDE, Deirdre was changed by the ordeal. While she had always exhibited a maturity and wisdom beyond her years, this became more pronounced following her illness. Though still young, she demonstrates an insight that is unnerving, and the certainty of her beliefs is astounding. She harbors no doubt whatsoever and *knows*—not believes, but *knows*—that God and Christ are always with her. Once when I was reminding her that she could always turn to Christ for help, she responded, somewhat irritably, "You don't have to tell me about Jesus," she said. "I met Him, remember? I know He's *always* right here with me. *Don't* keep telling me about what I already know!"

She rarely refers to her visit to the akashic records or any information she may recall from the several books she read. She believes that she can remember information when it is necessary, however, and she is certain that God is directing her path.

Deirdre's path had never been an easy one, and that has not changed. If anything, it has become more difficult. Differences between her and her peers have grown, and she has lost a part of her childhood that she will never recover. During one particularly difficult time, she chided me for not understanding how hard it had been for her. She said that when she returned from "heaven," she knew she couldn't be a little girl any more.

"I had to put away my dolls and toys," she said. "They didn't seem important any more. There was so much I had to get ready for, so much I have to do. It wasn't fair! You don't know how much that hurt!"

I thought back and remembered that the Barbie® dolls which had given her so many imaginative hours of joyful play had long been packed away in a box and placed in her closet. It seemed that despite Tino's and my efforts to the contrary, Deirdre's childhood had ended the day she came back to us. We had lost our daughter, in a sense, for the carefree little girl we knew was gone forever. The innocence of her childhood had been replaced by a determined spirit of purpose and inner knowing. Another path beckoned, and she had to answer that call. All we could do was be there for her and help her along the way.

TRANSFORMATIVE VISION: A CHANGE IN PERCEPTION

While Deirdre's near-death experience certainly had a profound effect upon her, the miracle which surrounded that experience affected others as well, as it altered our perception and consciousness by expanding our paradigms.

Paradigms. In science, a paradigm is the framework or reference point by which we analyze incoming stimuli. It establishes the boundaries for our beliefs, gives us rules for successful behavior, filters information received, and influences our perception. It is so powerful that experiments indicate that a researcher will disregard or even alter data that does not fit into the accepted paradigm.[3] Yet paradigms do change, and as they change so does our perception of the world.

For example, a widely accepted paradigm was the belief that the world was flat. For hundreds of years, people made judgments and assumptions based upon this erroneous paradigm. Sailors of the sea who told of distant lands and strange peoples were deemed insane and their information disregarded; it did not fit the accepted paradigm. After the voyage of Columbus, however, the fallacy of this paradigm was exposed, and humanity's perception of the world changed.

When Miracles Change Paradigms. The doctor who was worried about a number on a monitor initially ignored Deirdre's responsiveness because his paradigm said that she could not be responding. Dr. Chaves was speaking within the framework of his paradigm on the disease when he said that he couldn't believe Deirdre had recovered until he saw her walking and talking. His paradigm told him that, in light of her physical condition, death was the only possible outcome. When she defied this paradigm by living and recovering without brain damage or paralysis, it changed his perception and caused him to question his paradigm about the course and outcome of the disease. A miracle thus has the effect of changing paradigms, because it shows us an alternate reality we had not thought possible.

THE MIRACLE AS A LEARNING SITUATION

While Deirdre's miracle manifested as a spontaneous healing, there are times when—despite our faith, prayer, love, and genuine efforts—healing doesn't occur. In fact, one of the most puzzling mysteries surrounding miracles and healing is the question of why some people are healed and others are not.[4]

When Healing Doesn't Occur.   It is possible that there are times when the illness or the disability itself provides an opportunity for that soul to teach others or perhaps to learn a lesson itself. It may be that the soul has chosen, before birth, to accept a physical limitation so that it may teach others through this experience and, by doing so, move forward in its own spiritual progress. Think of the young child stricken by cancer who, despite his or her situation, still looks on life with joy and wonder. This child teaches us through the miracle of acceptance. What about the boy born with Down's syndrome, who strives to overcome his "handicap" and teaches us the true meaning of courage and triumph? Or the AIDS patient, whose suffering gives us the opportunity to learn love and compassion?

Since a miracle is a learning situation which provides an opportunity for spiritual growth, it may be expressed in different ways depending upon the lesson it seeks to teach. Yet whatever form the miracle takes, it serves to teach us to see beyond our limited human perception of reality. We, with our earthly eyes, cannot always see the total picture as Spirit can. All we can do is learn to trust that each circumstance, no matter its appearance, is an opportunity for spiritual growth which provides us with the chance to discover our true self and move us closer to a remembrance of our oneness with the Creative Force.

LIKE RIPPLES IN A POND

While this miracle was certainly a learning situation which changed those of us involved, it surprised us to learn of the many ways in which our miracle touched others. In the months following Deirdre's recovery, we often heard from people who wanted to share with us the way in which this experience touched their lives. Some people called or wrote to tell us what an inspiration it had been. Eric Knight, the son of family friends in Massachusetts, sent a card to Deirdre at least twice a week for the next two months. Some even sent gifts, and Deirdre unexpectedly received crystals, a "magic" amulet, and several books on Native Americans.

Many of these people were strangers to us when we began the journey, yet they, too, felt blessed by a lesson this miracle taught them. To some, the miracle was a wondrous healing, a message of hope which proved helpful when going through crises of their own. To others, it was the triumph of life over death and served as living proof that miracles do happen. Still others saw it as a remarkable demonstration of cooperation and understanding which grew between people of vastly different faiths—a lesson that, despite our differences, we can strive for and attain a higher level of spiritual awareness and tolerance toward our fellow human beings. And many others saw it also as providing a pattern or blueprint which would prove helpful in dealing with the difficulties of everyday life. Yet, however the miracle was perceived and no matter the lessons learned, there can be no doubt that it had a profound effect on all whom it touched.

LASTING LESSONS: EARTH SCHOOL IN SESSION

Universal Lessons. There were many lessons to be found in this earth-school session. It was not so much that it led us to new beliefs, but rather that it was a physical demonstration or visible proof that what we thought to be real *was real.* The lessons we learned validated our spiritual beliefs and demonstrated their truth. Some lessons seemed to be tailored to individual needs, while others had a more general or universal application. These so-called "universal" lessons taught us about spiritual beliefs and concepts and changed the way we would look at life. Here are what some of those lessons were:

1. *We are spiritual beings;* the body we inhabit is just a

shell which houses our soul while on the earth plane. Because we are eternal spiritual beings, there is no death.

2. Because our true being is spiritual, we can *harness our spiritual energy to effect change on the physical level.* This includes healing any physical, mental, or emotional condition. The power of prayer energy is real and can be used to effect change in the physical world.

3. *The universe operates according to divine or spiritual laws* which were established for the purpose of guiding us on our spiritual path back to oneness with the Universal Spirit. Once we align ourselves with universal law, we realize our true potential and take the first step toward reclaiming our birthright as co-creators with the God-Force.

4. *There are no accidents.* The situation in which you find yourself has happened for a reason. Seek to find that reason and learn from it. Your choices have helped to create your circumstance.

5. *Adversity is a learning situation.* Any problem, hurtful relationship, disease, injury, or other crisis should be seen not as an affliction, but as an opportunity for growth and transformation. A strong faith in a power greater than ourselves is necessary to sustain us in times of adversity. Faith enhances the power of prayer and gives it strength.

6. *God IS Love.* God does not love; God IS Love. Love defines all that God IS. God can be nothing else. Since God IS Love, love is the most powerful force in the universe. It has the ability to transform any and all situations.

7. *Healing is an attunement with the Creative Forces,* so healing must come from Love. Love is the great healer. It can heal any illness, relationship, or situation, be it physical, mental, emotional, or spiritual.

8. The wonder-working power of God can create miracles! Go beyond an intellectual acceptance of the possibility of a miracle and know in your heart that in God's world, *miracles are real!*

9. It's important to learn to *live in the now,* minute to

minute. Worrying about the past or the future will scatter your focus and drain your energy, making you unable to concentrate on the issue at hand.

Personal Lessons. While we all benefited from the universal lessons of this journey, there were also individual lessons destined to be met along the way. These "personal" lessons were directed to meet individual needs and situations, and often touched a life in a unique way.

As for me, I learned the importance of "letting go." I had always tried to be in control of every situation, but this time I found myself in the one situation upon which I could exert no control whatsoever. I had to learn to rely on others and let them do for me when I couldn't do for myself. Tino believes that he finally overcame the need to worry about things past and things future. He no longer is anxious about problems, for he knows they can be overcome since it is we who create them. Sharon described a similar lesson, saying that she learned the need to "live in the now" and only in the now moment. Dot came to know the true meaning of unconditional love, accepting people for who they are. Darcie learned the importance of perseverance, saying that she realized that "where there's life, there's hope." Brenda not only learned the power of love, but learned to accept it for herself. And Bill came to know the reality of miracles.

Reverend Mary Omwake, perhaps, had the most interesting lesson of all, for she learned that miracles often come in disguise. She shared with us the fact that she had nearly avoided making that first hospital call; she was so exhausted that she first thought to refer the call to an assistant minister at the church. Looking back, she realized how much she would have missed if she had not been the one to come. From that point on, she insisted that she attend to every crisis intervention request from the congregation. She learned that any situation, no matter how distressing it might appear, can hold the promise of a miracle.

THE RIPPLES SPREAD:
THE TESTIMONY OF OTHERS

While it was clear to us that this miracle held many lessons for many people, it is the testimony of others which best demonstrates the far-reaching effects of our miracle. Several such anecdotes deserve special mention here, for they are excellent examples of the different ways in which the ripples of this miracle fanned out to touch the lives of others.

Hope for Another. One of the first indications of the far-reaching ripple effect occurred during a situation with people who had not even been involved in our ordeal. The summer following Deirdre's illness, a navy service member at my command was seriously injured during a motorcycle accident. He was taken to a hospital in Topeka, Kansas, where he was comatose with an unknown prognosis. When I first heard about it, I knew that I had to go visit the family and in some small way return the many kindnesses that had been shown to us by so many people. I felt that for some reason, Deirdre had to go also. I asked Brenda to accompany me for moral support, and she and her daughter Sara came with us on the hour-plus drive to Topeka.

This hospital had quite a different atmosphere from UKMC, and at first the staff was reluctant to let non-family members see patients, although we were allowed to visit for a few minutes. Brenda and I returned to the waiting room to speak with the family, while Deirdre and Sara went for a soda. When I met his mother, June, I knew that she was the reason I had to come here. I told her all about Deirdre and what had happened. By the time I finished, she had tears in her eyes and, just as I ended, Deirdre walked into the room. She took Deirdre's hand and began to cry. After a few minutes she composed herself and thanked us profusely for coming and sharing our story. She said that she always believed in prayer and miracles, and that seeing Deirdre would help her hold on to her faith. She felt that our visit was a sign that her son would recover. I told her that we would keep them all in our prayers. Within another day her son did regain consciousness and, after several months of rehabilitation, was on the road to an excellent recovery.

I spoke to June some weeks later, and she again told me how much our visit had meant to her. This incident prompted me to ponder the potential effect Deirdre's story might have on people, and for the first time I realized that there might be a need to share it with others.

Facing Surgery. Unknown to us during Deirdre's illness, there was a prisoner's group at Fort Leavenworth, Kansas, who became involved in the prayer network. One member of the group continued to correspond with Darcie and later that year wrote to say that he was facing major surgery of his own, and the prognosis for recovery was not good. In his letter he asked that we pray for him and spoke of drawing inspiration and hope from his experience with Deirdre. He was afraid, but his involvement in the prayer network showed him that miraculous healing was possible, and he felt that through prayer he, too, could be healed and come through the surgery successfully. We did add him to our prayer list at this time and later received word that the surgery had been a success and that he was on his way to recovery.

A Case of Cancer. In 1992, more than a year after Deirdre's hospitalization, a woman in the Boston area was diagnosed with cervical cancer. She was a friend of Darcie's and had been involved in the prayer network. Upon learning that she had cancer, she relied upon both medical knowledge and spiritual means to effect a cure. In less than two months, her cancer was in remission, and she credited her knowledge of our experience with Deirdre in helping her keep her faith. She wrote about her experience in *Harvest,* a regional journal:

"I acted on the mundane (vitamins, herbs, doctor visit),

then I acted on the magical level (ritual, meditation). What kept me believing healing was possible was remembering the healing of Darcie's niece (Deirdre) that Darcie described in *Harvest*. If they could heal her, why couldn't I, with a little help from a small circle of friends, heal me? We could, and we did."[5]

Inspiration for a Nurse.   In March 1992, Deirdre was stopped by a woman at a school event. The woman asked her if she had been at Shawnee Mission Medical Center about a year ago. When Deirdre told her yes, that she'd had Reye's syndrome the year before, the woman explained that she was a nurse who had been on duty in the emergency room that night. This was the same nurse who had asked me to keep her informed on Deirdre's condition when she was being transferred to UKMC. She was the same nurse who called UKMC every day that Deirdre was in intensive care to check on her condition.

Somehow, a year later, she recognized Deirdre as the same little girl she had treated so many months before. She asked Deirdre if she could give her a hug, explaining that when she first saw her in emergency, she reminded her of her own daughter and, therefore, took a special interest in her. She told her to tell me (her mother) that she had prayed very hard for her and was very happy to see that she was doing so well. She also said that this experience helped her through other "hopeless" cases because she had seen that miracles do happen.

A Healing Ministry.   While this miracle most often had the effect of touching lives on an individual level, it also effected change at the group level. It served as the impetus for what would become a healing prayer ministry at Unity Church of Overland Park. Within weeks the Unity congregation began to direct its focus toward a more formal use of healing prayer, and a prayer group was formed. This group grew in size and commitment and now meets at noon six days a week, accepting prayer requests by phone or letter.

The church has earned a nationwide reputation for its "prayer power," and I am told that Mary still talks about the miracle healing of a little girl which first helped guide the church toward this calling.

A Case Study. Another somewhat unexpected group which continues to be affected by the miracle are the medical students enrolled at UKMC. I mentioned earlier that Deirdre's case had become part of the medical school curriculum at UKMC. It is cited as a most severe case of Reye's syndrome, characterized by a level of coma resulting in lack of cognitive brain activity with only low levels of basal brain function. The lack of brain activity combined with the brain edema indicated massive destruction of brain tissue and should have meant that death was imminent. Yet, for an unexplainable reason, the patient not only recovered, but quickly regained completely unimpaired brain activity and function.

The case is used to demonstrate to medical students that not all diseases follow the predicted etiology. UKMC wanted its future doctors to realize that there are times when a patient "ignores" the clinical prognosis and recovers, despite the fact that it is a medical impossibility. The case is used to show that not all instances fall within normal parameters; some do exceed established boundaries and defy rational explanation.

Although the teaching staff may not use the word "miracle," if even one medical school is teaching our future doctors that such "unexplainable" recoveries do occur, think what this could mean to a new generation of doctors If other medical schools are following similar procedures, think what an impact it could have on a new generation of medical healers.

THE MIRACLE CONTINUES: THE FINAL LESSON

We have already seen that the effects of a miracle are far

reaching and long lasting. The lessons that we learn and the information we gain from such an experience transform us and remain with us long after the incident which triggered the miracle has waned. The power of this transformation will continue as long as one applies what has been learned in all future circumstances.

The final lesson, then, was to glean all that we learned during our journey and formulate it into a workable plan of action that could be applied to any adversity which might arise in daily life. This process is firmly rooted in the principles of universal, spiritual law that have been mentioned previously. It can be used by anyone who is willing to see adversity as a growth opportunity, which helps that person to discover his or her true self.

Once you have accepted these precepts, you can begin to apply them to any situation. As you do so, you start moving from fear of crisis to anticipation of opportunity. You will find within you the inner resources needed to help change obstacles into stepping-stones, hardships into blessings, and transform crises into miracles. All you need to do is take that first step and enlist the following suggestions that helped create a miracle in my family:

1. Secure the aid of a support group. You cannot complete this process alone; the sheer physical exhaustion factor is too great. Know that when two or more people unite in the spirit of love to help another, there is *nothing* they cannot do! When people unite in thought and prayer, they create a powerful energy force that can be directed to effect change on the physical level.

2. Maintain a positive focus on the best possible outcome you can imagine. Affirm that it is now manifesting in your life.

3. Free your mind of all preconceptions and expectations. Learn to look beyond the illusion of the physical to the reality of the spirit. Don't accept worldly appearances as real.

4. Become an open channel through which the creative energy of Spirit can flow. Listen to your inner voice and allow Spirit to direct your actions.

5. Pray and meditate on the situation. Ask for guidance. Listen and act on the guidance you receive.

6. Share the information you receive with your support group. Exchange ideas and explore their meaning. Tune in to the energy being generated and pass it on amongst the others. It will grow in power and effect through cooperation.

7. Release the problem to a Higher Power in prayer, with faith, and in expectation of your highest ideal. Realize that even as you pray, it is being done!

8. Expect the miracle! Accept the outcome. Know that the creative God-Force always works to bring about the highest good for all concerned.

9. Share your experiences. For miracles, like knowledge, will grow and multiply only if shared with others. But remember, be careful not to force your beliefs on others.

FINAL STEPS

We lingered on this pinnacle for quite some time. There was much to reflect upon and consider. The brilliant light of the sun magnified our sight and enhanced our vision. Things which before seemed blurred and obscure appeared to be surprisingly clear and vivid. The serenity we felt gave us a sense of peace and knowing we had not experienced before. From this height, we saw the true beauty of the world and of ourselves. Yet something told us we could not stay here forever; it would soon be time to leave. There was other work to do.

But if we cannot stay, why bother to make the journey in the first place? We make the journey because the memory of what we saw remains with us. By reaching the summit, we lifted our vision above the finite beliefs of the world and freed ourselves of humanmade limitations. We beheld ourselves as we exist in God's truth and perfection. We beheld the truth of the world and understood that fear and doubt, disease and lack, are not things in themselves, but the absence of Spirit. We will never again forget these lessons, for through our journey, they have been ingrained into our very being. The lessons we learned on this hard-fought journey would continue to affect our lives, even as they radiated outward to touch the lives of others. Our final steps would be to remember the knowledge gained through these lessons, bring it back with us from the mountaintop, and learn to apply it to any future situation we might encounter as we continued the ultimate journey of life itself.

❋ ❋ ❋

You cannot stay on the summit forever; you have to come down again. So why bother in the first place? Because what is below does not know what is above, but what is above knows what is below.
—Mt. Analogue, *author anonymous*

Epilogue

The Road Goes Ever On

Roads go ever on and on, over rock and under tree,
By caves where never sun has shown, by streams that never
find the sea...
Yet feet that wandering have gone, turn at last to home
afar...

—Bilbo Baggins at the end of his journey
in *The Hobbit*, J.R.R. Tolkein

As the hobbit Bilbo Baggins finishes this poem at the end of a spectacular journey, Gandalf the Grey, a wizard of great power and knowledge, looks at him and says, "My dear, Bilbo! Something is the matter with you! You are not the hobbit that you were."[1] An understatement, to say the least, for Bilbo's adventures did change him, as such journeys often do.

But there comes the day when the traveler completes the

journey and looks toward home, anxious to resume familiar ways. Yet while outward appearances may return to normal, it is virtually certain that the traveler will never be the same, for the steps of the journey have changed him or her forever.

LIFE AFTER A MIRACLE

Prior to our terrifying and miraculous journey, we had been ordinary people leading ordinary lives, who, for a few brief moments, found ourselves caught up in extraordinary circumstances. Following the emotional upheavals of this tumultuous turn of events, we had no greater desire than to return to "normal" life as we knew it.

In the months following Deirdre's recovery, our lives slowly began to return to the routine rhythm of daily life. There was no magical, instantaneous change in our living conditions. Deirdre returned to school and Tino and I returned to our jobs. Our friends and family did the same. Once again, we found ourselves confronted with the trials and tribulations that everyday life brings. Both Deirdre and her friend Sara entered the adolescent years and faced the same problems as every other young teen-age girl. There were problems with jobs and economic difficulties. Life resumed the same patterns we had always known. We still faced the same ups and downs, the same highs and lows as everyone else moving along life's path. Although no crisis would ever reach the epic proportions we had seen during Deirdre's illness, we still experienced difficulties and sorrow.

Although I received a year's extension of my naval assignment in Kansas, I had to transfer to New England in March of 1992. This was perhaps the most difficult move we had ever made and, at times, we wondered if we had made the right decision. Yet despite the miles which separated us, the bonds we had formed with our study group family actually grew stronger as we discovered that we could still be there for one another despite the distance. We were only a phone call away, and prayer, we knew, could help at any distance. The separation forced us to become stronger and, because of the move, I had the opportunity to join a new study group and meet people who have become valued friends. (A.R.E. study groups exist throughout the United States and abroad.)

Challenges came not only from the mundane difficulties life sent our way, but from the personal loss and feeling of sorrow and pain that come when a loved one leaves the earth plane. Since Deirdre's miracle, we lost both her beloved uncle Wilbur, and my dear aunt and godmother Ida. Brenda said good-by to her father. Although we knew they had gone on to a higher spiritual plane, it did not lessen our sense of loss or the regret that we couldn't share their lives a bit longer.

Thus, from all outward appearances our lives were no different from those of any other ordinary group of people. To look at us, no one would have imagined that a short time before, we had been actively involved in witnessing a miracle of life over death. Yet there had been a change— and a significant one at that—because a miracle works changes from within: while outward appearances remained the same and the challenges of everyday life continued, our responses to those challenges had changed.

A New Outlook on Life

Because of the trials we had faced during our journey, we found that we were able to face challenges and adversity with a new-found sense of inner peace, calm, and resolve. Adversity *had* proved to be a path of growth. Just as a broken bone which, once healed, is stronger than the surrounding bone which was not broken, we had "become strong in the broken places."[2]

It was as if we intuitively knew that whatever the situation, we could rise above the momentary doubt, fear, and pain and find in it a knowledge which would bring us closer to our spiritual source. We no longer "sweated the little things" and have come to realize that any adversity, no matter its appearance, is a "little thing" when faced with the help of God. We no longer rush headlong toward the future because we know that life is unfolding as it should. We are working to reach the point where we can thank the Universal Spirit for everything that it sets before us, knowing that any problem, difficult situation, bad relationship, or crisis, when seen as a learning situation, can be transformed into an opportunity for growth, and yes, even a miracle. For we had learned to look beyond human perceptions and see with the eyes of Spirit.

Seeing through the eyes of Spirit requires a shift in perception as we learn to see *through* the mind rather than *with* it. We learn to look beyond the illusory veils of limiting paradigms which say "can't" and expand our frame of reference to include those paradigms which say "with Spirit, I can."

Once your perception has changed, you understand that there are no bad experiences. Each experience life sends our way has a valuable lesson to offer if we but look beyond outward appearances and seek the truth within. Every challenge becomes an opportunity in disguise, to be met with love and understanding, for you know that if you can work your way through it, it will hold a meaningful lesson. Remember that we are only presented with a lesson when we are ready to learn it. You already possess within yourself everything you need in order to meet this challenge successfully; you need only apply what you already know.

"Our Conscious Self will never know what serves our highest good or the good of the whole. We can come to trust in what life offers with faith in the inherent wisdom, meaning, and perfection of all that occurs."[3]

A STRANGE AND WONDROUS THING

Once you have been touched by a miracle, your life will be changed, although we may never fully understand how a miracle works its wonders. Perhaps it is enough, as Albert Einstein thought, to recognize the miracle without understanding its mystery. "The beauty of it is that we have to content ourselves with the recognition of the miracle, beyond which there is no legitimate way out."[4]

As I was making the final editorial changes on this book, I received a letter from Jan Snyder, the "medicine woman" who had visited Deirdre during her illness. I hadn't had any contact with her since that time, and she wondered if I would remember her! She found out that this book was going to be published and wanted to wish me well. I share her words with you here, for I believe they echo the sentiments of many involved in this, our miracle:

"Yours is a wonderful, inspiring, powerful story. I'm glad it's being told so that others will know that all things are possible through prayer, so that others will understand how powerful individual and collective focus really is. That miracle had a great impact on my life. I reflect on what I know and saw and felt and am always humbled by the delicate weaving and sheer force of it all."

The miracle is a gift of Spirit that allows you to manifest your highest spiritual ideals through the application of conscious forces and actions in the material plane. It is a teaching device which accelerates our learning by lifting the veil of illusion the physical world imposes and restoring our clarity of vision so that we can see the truth of our spiritual being. It changes our perception and helps us to expand beyond our self-imposed limits and realize that nothing is impossible. It teaches us to look beyond illusion to reality and see the beauty which exists in each and every moment, and empowers us to see each moment as an opportunity to create something positive.

A miracle *is* a most strange and wondrous thing. A miracle can manifest when and where you least expect it. It is not something to be understood or analyzed, but something which must be experienced or believed in the heart. "For those who believe no proof is necessary. For those who don't believe, no proof is possible."[5]

THE SPIRITUAL PATH

I believe that all souls have an innate desire to find the spiritual path which will lead them back to a conscious realization of their "at-one-ment" with the Spiritual Source or God. A spiritual path is found when you set aside all selfish motives of greed, self-gain, or glory and strive to be of *loving service to others* by demonstrating love, mercy, forgiveness, and understanding to all those you meet. I also believe that no one owns an exclusive copyright on the "right" spiritual path. God created us as individual beings endowed with free will. Our past experiences also affect the way we view ourselves and our relationship to the universe. What rings true for one person may hold no value for another. You must look into your heart and find the key that will awaken your soul memory of the spiritual being you really are and use that key to unlock the door which separates you from the spiritual path leading to oneness with God.

One person's path may lie in a life dedicated to monastic studies; another's path may lie in unselfish service as a teacher or doctor. Yet another person may find the path through the little kindnesses unselfishly done every day. The bus driver whose smile makes each morning a little brighter for the passengers or the crossing guard who says a kind word to schoolchildren as they begin the day are both actively following the path.

But no matter how you find it, you will soon learn that the spiritual path is not an easy one to follow. It is sometimes much easier to be carried away by the whims of the crowd in the physical world than to allow our true spiritual nature to show through. It is easier to stay with the familiar than to explore the unknown. The learning opportunities that may present themselves on the spiritual path can be hard lessons to learn, and many turn away before they even begin. Hence the spiritual path is considered "the road less traveled." But be warned, for once you set your foot upon this path, it is difficult to turn away, for you have seen a glimpse of what can be and you will never be satisfied with less again.

I know this is certainly true for me. Each time I wonder why I chose the path I did and wish for an easier life devoid of such "wonderful" learning opportunities, the still, small voice within reminds me that, after having seen what is on the mountaintop, I would not be content with anything less. When I remember the pain and anguish I endured during my daughter's illness, I think I would have done anything to avoid the situation despite the fact that she recovered. Yet, when I see the ramifications of this miracle and think of how many people have been touched by it, I wonder how I could even think of missing this opportunity of a lifetime.

Is it any surprise that one of Deirdre's favorite poems, "The Road Not Taken" by the American poet Robert Frost, expresses this very sentiment:

"Two roads diverged in a wood, and I—/I took the one less traveled by,/And that has made all the difference."

Once you choose the road less traveled, it *will* make all the difference. But what a magnificent difference it will be, for you will find your true self.

From Sorrow to Joy

Years ago, when Deirdre was baptized, the minister asked

me the meaning of her name, saying that he liked to link the meaning with a scripture quotation during the baptism. When I told him that Deirdre was an Irish name derived from the mythological princess "Deirdre of the Sorrows," he seemed perplexed. I knew he was wondering what good he could find to say about sorrow. After a moment's pause, he suddenly grinned and said triumphantly, "I've got it! '...your sorrow shall be turned into joy.'" (John 16:20)

Little did I know how prophetic those words would prove to be. Just as the tragic death of that legendary princess had the unforeseen blessing of uniting all of Ireland and ending generations of war, so, too, did we see blessings arise out of the ashes of adversity. Ten years later our greatest sorrow would indeed become our greatest joy. Coincidence? Perhaps. Or a portent of things to come? We can only wonder.

It is my hope that you have been able to share in some small part of that joy and the wonder it has brought into our lives. Our miracle journey has shown us that many, many people think as we do and believe in the presence of angels, the power of prayer and love, the reality of miracles, and the truth of a spiritual life beyond the death of the physical body. If any part of our journey echoes true in your heart, take it, apply it, and use it as you see fit. May you know that you, too, have within you the power to transform a crisis into a miracle.

JOURNEY'S END

And so ended our journey. We had traversed a long and winding road, descending through valleys of deep desolation and ascending to heights of great beauty. Now it was over; we had returned home. Yet the lessons we learned were forever etched upon the skein of time and space, so that all who wish may learn from them.

There are many paths which lead us to a closer oneness with God. The path which may be right for one person may not be right for another. Yet each path brings the traveler to new heights through a process of challenge, learning, and understanding. As miracles occur along the path, vast distances can be covered with the taking of a small step. If travelers persevere, they will be rewarded with knowledge found only at the mountain's top, knowledge which they can take with them and apply to other paths as they travel along life's journey.

For there is really only one journey that continues still— the journey of the soul as it seeks to remember its spiritual origins and return home. Someday this journey will be over, too, as we all remember our true state of oneness with God. But until then, we must keep seeking to know the truth and strive to stay on the spiritual path that is set before us. But be warned, for once you embark upon the spiritual path, you will never be content with anything less. You may stray from the path, but you will always heed the call to return. The adventures you encounter may stretch you to your limits and beyond, but it is only by exceeding your perceived limits that you will find your true self. Celebrate the wonder of this journey, and rejoice that it will lead you home.

* * *

Second star to the right and on till morning.
—Captain James T. Kirk, giving orders for the final voyage of the USS *Enterprise,* echoing Peter Pan's directions to Never-Never Land

Endnotes

Foreword

1. Bill Moyers, *Healing and the Mind,* Doubleday, New York, 1993.
2. Cousins Norman, ed., *The Physician in Literature,* W.B. Saunders, Philadelphia, 1982.

Prologue: *Spirit in Action*

1. *Webster's New World Dictionary of the American Language, sub verbo* "crisis," p. 149.
2. For purposes of this book, the terms God, God-Force, God-Presence, Creative Force, Universal Mind, and Spirit are all used interchangeably to represent the universal spiritual source of all creation.
3. A traditional, although somewhat vague, definition of *metaphysics* is: that esoteric branch of philosophy which deals with first principles and ultimate grounds, causation, and the relation of universals to particulars (*The Random House Dictionary of the English Language,* 2nd edition, unabridged, *sub verbo* "metaphysics," p. 1208). I, however, prefer to use a more workable definition: the study of the cause-and-effect relationship between spirit or energy and the physical or material.
4. Emmet Fox, *The Mental Equivalent,* p. 4.
5. The Jewish cabala is a complex system of thought and practice based upon metaphysical principles. As early as 180 A.D., the Christian scholar Origen taught metaphysical symbology. Other early Christian mystics include St. Francis of Assisi, Jacob Boehme, and Meister Eckhart. In terms of Scripture, some authorities consider the Book of the Revelation by St. John the Disciple to be a classic metaphysical text written after a profound meditation.
6. Dozens of books have been written on the life and work of Edgar Cayce. A recommended biography is *There Is a River,* by Thomas Sugrue, available through the A.R.E. Press.

7. Gary Zukav, *The Seat of the Soul*, p. 234.

8. For a detailed discourse on the universal laws and their application, see *Your Life: Why It Is the Way It Is and What You Can Do About It*, by Bruce McArthur.

9. As used here, Jesus the Christ is taken to be the highest manifestation of God on earth, for, as Jesus of Nazareth, He was in complete "at-one-ment" with the Father and thus achieved the Christhood.

10. *A Course in Miracles*, Foundation for Inner Peace, 1975.

Chapter One: *The Journey Begins*

1. *Closer to the Light*, Melvin Morse, M.D.

2. For more information on the subject of creative visualization see *Creative Visualization*, by Shakti Gawain.

Chapter Two: *Prayer in Action*

1. Reading 281-13.

2. Reading 731-1.

3. Reading 496-1.

4. Reading 281-9.

5. Randolph Byrd, M.D., "Positive Therapeutic Effects of Intercessory Prayer in a Coronary Care Unit Population," *Southern Medical Journal*, July 1988.

6. Eric Butterworth, "The Way of the Silence," *Unity*, January 1993, p. 19.

7. As quoted in *Awaken the Giant Within*, Anthony Robbins, p. 409.

8. Reading 2981-1.

9. Charles Fillmore, "The Healing Power of Joy," *Unity*, June 1994, p. 59.

Chapter Three:
Step by Step: Guidance Through Dreams and Meditation

1. Jonathan Star, *Two Suns Rising: An Anthology of Eastern and Western Mystical Writings*, Bantam, 1991, p. 224.

2. George Lucas, *The Star Wars: From the Adventures of*

Luke Skywalker, Ballantine, 1986.
   3. Reading 281-13.
   4. Reading 281-41.
   5. Reading 262-89.
   6. The belief in past lives or reincarnation, as used here, refers to the belief that the soul may live more than one lifetime in human form. It does *not* include the Hindu belief of transmigration, which states that a soul may inhabit an animal body. Those desiring more information on the topic of reincarnation may consult the following books: *Edgar Cayce on Reincarnation* by Noel Langley; *Many Happy Returns* by W.H. Church; *Many Lives, Many Masters* by Brian Weiss; and *Beyond the Ashes* by Rabbi Yonassan Gershom.
   7. Reincarnation implies the concept of karma. Simply stated, karma is the belief that whatever you create as a result of your thoughts, words, and actions—good or bad, in this lifetime or another—comes back to you. Karmic law operates under the law of cause and effect, which states that for every action (cause), there is a reaction (effect). It parallels the idea of "as you sow, so shall you reap." (Galatians 6:7) Karma in this sense does not judge; you simply reap or meet the effects of your own actions. Even so-called "bad karma," however, works for our good, for it teaches us the lessons we have entered this life to learn. By understanding karma as a law of balance, we begin to learn from karmic conditions and use them as a means of positive change in our lives. By meeting such conditions with forgiveness and love, we move beyond the law of karma to the law of grace.
   8. Anthony Robbins, *Awaken the Giant Within,* p. 189.

Chapter Four: *Faith in Action*
   1. Bruce McArthur, *Your Life: Why It Is the Way it Is and What You Can Do About It,* pp. 232 and 237.
   2. James Coyle Morgan, *Jesus and Mastership,* Oakbridge University Press, Federal Way, Washington.

Chapter Five: *Healers One and All*

1. Pesach Krauss and Morrie Goldfischer, *Why Me? Coping with Grief, Loss, and Change*, p. iv.
2. Reading 262-104.
3. Frank Waters, *The Book of the Hopi*, p. 9.
4. The formula for this oil consisted primarily of peanut oil, olive oil, and lanolin.
5. Reading 3659-1.
6. Reading 281-29.

Chapter Six: *Love in Action*

1. *A Search for God*, Book I, "Love," p. 124.
2. Bruce McArthur, *Your Life: Why It Is the Way It Is and What You Can Do About It*, p. 249.
3. As quoted by Anthony Robbins in *Awaken the Giant Within*, p. 531.
4. Frances Vaughn, M.D., "The Heart of Healing," *Radiant Health*, p. 12.
5. Siegel, Bernie S., *Love, Medicine, and Miracles*, pp. 181, 225, and 6.
6. Larry Dossey, M.D., *Healing Words*, p. 3.
7. *Twelve Steps and Twelve Traditions*, p. 34.
8. *A Search for God*, Book II, "Day and Night," p. 154.
9. See *The Complete Essays of Mark Twain*, Charles Neider, editor.
10. Readings 275-19 and 2533-8.

Chapter Ten: *Reflections from the Mountaintop*

1. James Redfield, *The Celestine Prophecy*, back cover.
2. See Melvin Morse, M.D., *Closer to the Light.*
3. Joel Barker, *Rediscovering the Future: On the Business of Paradigms* (videotape).
4. For an interesting discussion of case studies where healing involving "holy" men did not occur, consult "God in the Laboratory: A Look at Science, Prayer, and Healing," *The Healing Process*, Larry Dossey, M.D., pp. 30-31.

5. "Letters to the Editor," *Harvest,* Vol. 12, No. 7, 1992.

Epilogue: *The Road Goes Ever On*
1. J.R.R. Tolkein, *The Hobbit,* p. 284.
2. Dr. Bernie Siegel, lecture, as quoted in "Resource for Healing," by Rachel Remen, M.D., *The Healing Process,* p. 20.
3. Dan Millman, *No Ordinary Moments,* p. 287.
4. As quoted in "God in the Laboratory: A Look at Science, Prayer, and Healing," *The Healing Process,* Larry Dossey, M.D., p. 33.
5. John and Lyn St. Clair-Thomas, *Eyes of the Beholder* (as quoted in *A Guide for the Advanced Soul,* by Susan Hayward), p. 53.

Selected References

Butterworth, Eric. "The Way of the Silence." *Unity,* Vol. 173, No. 1, January 1993.

Course in Miracles, A. Tiburon, California: Foundation for Inner Peace, 1975.

Dossey, Larry, M.D. "God in the Laboratory: A Look at Science, Prayer, and Healing." *The Healing Process.* Unity Village, Missouri: Unity School of Christianity, 1992.

Dossey, Larry, M.D. *Healing Words.* San Francisco: Harper-Collins Publishers, 1993.

Fillmore, Charles. "The Healing Power of Joy." *Unity,* Vol. 174, No. 6, June 1994.

Fox, Emmet. *The Mental Equivalent.* Unity Village, Missouri: Unity School of Christianity, 1982.

Gawain, Shakti. *Creative Visualization.* San Rafael, California: New World Library, 1978.

Hayward, Susan. *A Guide for the Advanced Soul.* Avalon Beach, NSW, Australia: In-Tune Books, 1984.

Krauss, Pesach, and Goldfischer, Morrie. *Why Me? Coping with Grief, Loss, and Change.* New York: Bantam Books, 1990.

Lucas, George. *Star Wars* (movie).

McArthur, Bruce. *Your Life: Why It Is the Way It Is and What You Can Do About It.* Virginia Beach, Virginia: A.R.E. Press, 1993.

Millman, Dan. *No Ordinary Moments.* Tiburon, California: H.J. Kramer, Inc., 1992.

Morse, Melvin, M.D. *Closer to the Light: Learning from Near-Death Experiences of Children.* New York: Villard Books, 1990.

Redfield, James. *The Celestine Prophecy.* Hoover, Ala.: Satori Publishing, 1992.

Remen, Rachel, M.D. "Resource for Healing." *The Healing Process.* Unity Village, Missouri: Unity School of Christianity, 1992.

Robbins, Anthony. *Awaken the Giant Within: How to Take Immediate Control of Your Mental, Emotional, Physical, and Financial Destiny.* New York: Summit Books, 1991.

Rowland, May. *The Magic of the Word.* Unity Village, Missouri: Unity Books, 1972.

St. Clair-Thomas, John and Lyn. *Eyes of the Beholder.* Angel Publications, 1982.

Search for God, A, Books I and II. Virginia Beach, Virginia: A.R.E. Press, 1992 (anniversary edition).

Siegel, Bernie S., M.D. *Love, Medicine, and Miracles.* New York: HarperCollins, 1986.

Tolkien, J.R.R. *The Hobbit.* New York: Ballantine Books, 1973.

Twelve Steps and Twelve Traditions. New York: A.A. World Services, Inc., 1953.

Vaughn, Frances, M.D. "The Heart of Healing." *Radiant Health.* Unity Village, Missouri: Unity School of Christianity, 1993.

Waters, Frank. *The Book of the Hopi.* New York: The Viking Press, 1963.

Zukav, Gary. *The Seat of the Soul.* New York: Simon & Schuster, Inc., 1989.

Prayer Resources

The following is a list of prayer resource groups who can be contacted for specific prayer requests. Prayer requests can address any need, condition, or situation. There is no charge for these services and all prayer requests are kept confidential.

A.R.E. Glad Helpers. Meets each Wednesday from 9:00 a.m. to noon. Address requests to A.R.E. Prayer Services, P.O. Box 595, Virginia Beach, VA 23451-0595, or call (804) 428-3588.

Silent Unity. Provides a twenty-four-hour prayer vigil on a daily basis. Address requests to: Silent Unity, Unity Village, MO 64065 or call (816) 246-5400. *(If you have an urgent need and have no means of paying, you may call Silent Unity toll free: 1-800-669-7729.)*

Unity Church of Overland Park. Prayer Group meets Monday through Saturday at noon. Address prayer requests to: Unity Church of Overland Park, 9777 Antioch, Overland Park, KS 66212. The *Heartline* phone service provides uplifting prayers and affirmations, recorded daily. Call: (913) 649-3214.

Unity Church, Worldwide. This congregation provides a prayer ministry which accepts all prayer requests. Address those to: Prayer Department, Unity Church, Worldwide, P.O. Box 1709, Palm Desert, CA 92261-9989.

Study Group Resources

For information about A.R.E. study groups meeting in your area, contact the Study Group Department at A.R.E. headquarters in Virginia Beach, Virginia. Write to: A.R.E. Study Group Department, P.O. Box 595, Virginia Beach, VA 23451-0595, or call (804) 428-3588.

About the Author

Kathy L. Callahan, Ph.D., was born in Chicago, Illinois, and received a bachelor's degree from the University of Illinois at Chicago Circle. As a graduate student, she traveled to Tucson, Arizona, where she completed an assessment study of alcoholism treatment modalities for urban Papago Indians. She received a master's degree and Ph.D. from Purdue University.

An officer in the U.S. Navy since 1982, she served as a technical instructor at the Massachusetts Institute of Technology. She has also presented lectures on alcoholism and written numerous technical papers.

A longtime member of the Association for Research and Enlightenment, Inc., she strives to actively apply the principles found in the Edgar Cayce readings in her daily life. Her book, *Unseen Hands and Unknown Hearts: A Miracle of Healing Created Through Prayer,* is based on her personal experience of a miraculous healing that occurred when her daughter contracted a life-threatening disease—Reye's syndrome—in 1991.

She resides in Westborough, Massachusetts, with her husband, Tino Aragon, their daughter, Deirdre, and the family dog, Spirit.

What Is A.R.E.?

The Association for Research and Enlightenment, Inc. (A.R.E.®), is the international headquarters for the work of Edgar Cayce (1877-1945), who is considered the best-documented psychic of the twentieth century. Founded in 1931, the A.R.E. consists of a community of people from all walks of life and spiritual traditions, who have found meaningful and life-transformative insights from the readings of Edgar Cayce.

Although A.R.E. headquarters is located in Virginia Beach, Virginia—where visitors are always welcome—the A.R.E. community is a global network of individuals who offer conferences, educational activities, and fellowship around the world. People of every age are invited to participate in programs that focus on such topics as holistic health, dreams, reincarnation, ESP, the power of the mind, meditation, and personal spirituality.

In addition to study groups and various activities, the A.R.E. offers membership benefits and services, a bimonthly magazine, a newsletter, extracts from the Cayce readings, conferences, international tours, a massage school curriculum, an impressive volunteer network, a retreat-type camp for children and adults, and A.R.E. contacts around the world. A.R.E. also maintains an affiliation with Atlantic University, which offers a master's degree program in Transpersonal Studies.

For additional information about A.R.E. activities hosted near you, please contact:

A.R.E.
67th St. and Atlantic Ave.
P.O. Box 595
Virginia Beach, VA 23451-0595
(804) 428-3588

A.R.E. Press

A.R.E. Press is a publisher and distributor of books, audiotapes, and videos that offer guidance for a more fulfilling life. Our products are based on, or are compatible with, the concepts in the psychic readings of Edgar Cayce.

We especially seek to create products which carry forward the inspirational story of individuals who have made practical application of the Cayce legacy.

For a free catalog, please write to A.R.E. Press at the address below or call toll free 1-800-723-1112. For any other information, please call 804-428-3588.

A.R.E. Press
Sixty-Eighth & Atlantic Avenue
P.O. Box 656
Virginia Beach, VA 23451-0656